THE STORY

The Story of Theology

by

R. A. FINLAYSON

Professor of Systematic Theology,
Free Church College, Edinburgh

LONDON
THE TYNDALE PRESS
39 BEDFORD SQUARE, W.C.1

First Edition - - - December, 1963
Second Edition - - - June, 1969

STANDARD BOOK NUMBER 85111 029 0

Made and Printed in England by
Green & Co. (Lowestoft) Ltd., Crown Street, Lowestoft.

CONTENTS

	INTRODUCTION	7
I.	TERTULLIAN AND THE DOCTRINE OF THE TRINITY	13
II.	ATHANASIUS AND THE PERSON OF CHRIST	19
III.	AUGUSTINE AND THE DOCTRINE OF MAN	26
IV.	ANSELM AND THE DOCTRINE OF THE ATONEMENT	34
V.	LUTHER AND THE DOCTRINE OF JUSTIFICATION BY FAITH ALONE	42
VI.	CALVIN AND THE DOCTRINE OF AUTHORITY	48
VII.	SCHLEIERMACHER AND THE DOCTRINES OF MODERN THEOLOGY	56

INTRODUCTION

WE Christians of the twentieth century, who take the great doctrines of the faith for granted, rarely realize what it cost to secure them for us in the form in which we now have them, the care and deep insight, the struggle and conflict even unto blood, involved in formulating these doctrines and giving them expression in language that made it possible to hand them to posterity.

It is not that the Christian faith did not exist before the formulation of doctrine took place: on the contrary, these great truths were held by all Christians in the immediacy of faith; they were believed and cherished for personal salvation and spiritual comfort. But that was not enough if the faith was to remain in the possession of the Church. It must be clarified and fixed in a reasoned statement.

The necessity to think out its faith was thrust upon the Church by hostile forces that attacked it from without and by philosophies which undermined it from within. And the battle opened at a very early age, before the New Testament writings had been collected or the Canon of Scripture determined. It is very remarkable, therefore, that there should have been at so early a period so many attempts to state the faith as the necessity arose. And there is the scarcely less remarkable fact that the necessity arose in exactly the order in which we could reasonably expect it. This has resulted in a reasoned development of doctrine along lines that have continued to command the intellectual allegiance of students of the faith in every age.

By development of doctrine we mean there has been a gradual unfolding and formulation of the doctrine in the New Testament as the human mind applied itself to the material furnished in the divine revelation. This historical development will be seen to follow the logical order that renders it scientific as well as historical (see James Orr, *The Progress of Dogma*).

Christianity began with the witness to Jesus as the Son of God, and the deity of Christ remained the citadel of its faith, its most distinctive testimony according to its critics and defenders alike. But this belief carried implications that had soon to be faced.

The early Christians, in face of idolatry and polytheism, held tenaciously to the doctrine of the one only, the living and true God. They were avowed monotheists. But obviously if Christ was divine, and there was proclaimed to be but one only true God, some reasonable explanation must be given of the sense in which God was one, and of the place which Christ and the Holy Spirit occupied in the unity of the Godhead. Thus arose the necessity to formulate the doctrine of the Trinity, thrust upon the Church by its faith in the deity of Christ and the Person of the Spirit.

No sooner had the doctrine of a tri-personal God been formulated than questions arose as to the place of the God-Man Christ Jesus in the Trinity, the reality of His human and divine natures, and the relation between them. Thus, in the early fourth century, the Church was forced to direct its thought to the formulation of the doctrine of the Person of Christ, true God and true Man.

When the more objective doctrines of the faith had received attention, and there was leisure to turn to the more subjective aspects, inevitably man in his relation to God both as creature and as sinner came under discussion, involving a formulation not only of the doctrine of man, but of the doctrines of sin and grace. The doctrine of sin, on the other hand, gave urgency to the consideration of the doctrine of salvation, and so, a few centuries later, the doctrine of atonement came to be formulated.

When the Church had clarified its faith in the doctrine of atonement it became necessary to set forth the way of salvation and how the redemption wrought by Christ could be applied to man and become an experience in his life. This led to the formulation of the doctrine of salvation, at the heart of which lay the doctrine of justification by faith alone. As these foundation truths of the Christian faith found expression in creeds and confessions, they inevitably met with opposition and denials, not only from cold rationalism from without, but from sacerdotalism and formality from within. This threw the Church back on its authority for its faith, and the doctrine of Scripture and its authority for faith and life had to be discussed.

In all this there can be seen, as already indicated, not only a logical order, but a natural historical development. That is to say, the order in which the faith, as a matter of historical fact, came to be formulated followed that which the sequence of truth in the realm of faith indicated. Each doctrine could be formulated only in the light of the one that went before. There was thus a building up from the foundations, stone upon stone, and pillar upon pillar, till the whole edifice was erected.

There remains to be noted the very singular fact, around which the following pages take shape, that as each doctrine came to be discussed, there arose a man who possessed the convictions, the clarity of mind, and the force of character, to recognize the issues involved and to formulate a statement of them that commanded the consent of most of his fellow-Christians. Thus it is that the formulation of each of the great doctrines of the faith can be associated with one particular person who became the spokesman for the faith and convictions of the Christian Church. And so we have Tertullian and the doctrine of the Trinity, Athanasius and the doctrine of the Person of Christ, Augustine and the doctrine of man in sin and grace, Anselm and the doctrine of atonement, Luther and the doctrine of justification by faith alone, Calvin and the doctrine of authority. It is true that in none of these cases was the work done by one man alone. Each of the theologians mentioned entered into the labours of his predecessors in the same field, and those who came after made their own contribution to the doctrine now in possession of the Church. Nevertheless it remains true that God, in His wise providence, had His man ready, with the intellectual and spiritual equipment necessary, for the task to be done, and that the Church of all ages is debtor to those who, with such patience and vision and fidelity, gave reasoned expression to the faith once for all delivered to the saints.

Though the history of doctrine seems to bear out that the age of creed-making coincides with those times of religious awakening and spiritual quickening of which the Reformation is the great example in the Western Church, it has been thought expedient, in the second edition of this summary of historical development, to sketch out briefly the principal developments from the mid-eighteenth century to the present day, concentrating in the main on what has become known as the period of Modern Theology.

While several features of this theological development show some general similarity in approach and methodology, it is nevertheless apparent that there is also wide diversity in the conclusions reached and that the end-product can, in each case, be associated with a creative mind that dominated the theological thought of the period. To a greater extent than ever each phase of this development can be designated a personal theology rather than one embraced by the Church at large, or even by a recognizable segment of it.

It has often been observed that theology moves by a zig-zag route along the lines of action and reaction, like the swing of the pendulum. A case can be made out for the claim that it was so from the dawn of Christianity. Three theological positions can be discerned throughout the Christian centuries, evangelicalism, rationalism and sacerdotalism.

For instance we find that though the New Testament faith began as evangelicalism, very soon it was confronted by rationalism in the form of Gnosticism. Then sacerdotalism entered in to introduce its own forms and ceremonies in an attempt to crystallize the vital truths of the faith and so preserve them from extinction. Thus the ritualism of the fourth and fifth centuries was the Church's defence against the ravages of Gnostic rationalism.

Then again, for a full century after the Reformation, evangelicalism held sway, but in the seventeenth and eighteenth centuries it was countered by rationalism in the form of Deism and naturalistic philosophy. This period, it is significant, also marked the rise of ritualism under Laud. The Tractarian movement at a somewhat later date also arose under similar circumstances.

This would seem to be the pattern that theology is passing through in modern times. When evangelicalism has been weakening, or perhaps sheltering in an arid supernaturalism, rationalism reappears under the guise of modern theology, and when faith is sapped by rationalism, ritualism comes to the rescue, as in modern sacramentarianism, which, in order to bypass rationalism, places the essence of Christianity in symbolism and ritual. When Liberalism in theology had become mere rationalism at the close of the nineteenth century, many Christian thinkers took fright, even though they were submerged in it themselves. One of these was Karl Barth who early in his ministry sensed the utter bankruptcy of the Modernism given him to preach. We can discern in his case a violent swing of the pendulum towards a supernaturalism that surpassed anything known in Reformed theology before. That undoubtedly has had a tonic effect on a decadent Church and a diseased theology. But the swing of the pendulum was again inevitable, and this time it swung from Barthian hyper-supernaturalism through existentialism into the present-day position of secular theology. Whether a new emergence of sacerdotalism, in addition to what has been already working alongside Liberalism since the days of Bishop Gore, is the theological answer remains to be seen.

But the way also remains open for a more salutary reaction — a return to a truly biblical evangelicalism. It is hoped that this brief introduction to the story of theology will both bring home to us the debt we owe to those in previous generations, and enable us to do fuller justice in our own day to the deposit of truth given to us in the Scriptures.

BOOKS FOR GENERAL STUDY

James Orr, *The Progress of Dogma* (Eerdmans, 1962).

C. F. H. Henry (Ed.), *Basic Christian Doctrines* (Holt, Renelant and Winston, 1962).

CHAPTER I

TERTULLIAN AND THE DOCTRINE OF THE TRINITY

AS indicated in our introductory survey, it is clear that the doctrine of God as Father, Son, and Holy Ghost had occupied the mind of the Church from the first, even when the main emphasis had been placed on the personality and oneness of Deity. The revelation of God as a tri-unity is contained in the Scriptures as a progressive unfolding, and the formulation of the doctrine shared, for good historical reasons, in this progressive development. In the nature of things, amid the debasing influence of paganism and polytheism, the call was to proclaim the one living and true God. Not only so, but the early Christians themselves, so recently rescued from idolatry, were scarcely prepared to discuss the possibility that there might be a plurality of Persons in the Godhead. While they held tenaciously to the oneness of God and to the deity of Christ, they scarcely allowed themselves to ask how these two elements in their faith could be reconciled. Strange as this may seem to our modern consciousness, the reason for it is not far to seek. For them the oneness of God marked the dividing line between Christianity and paganism, and anything that imperilled this new-found faith had to be dismissed. In their discussions with non-Christians and with pagan teachers they were careful to stress God's omnipotence and universal sovereignty, and they introduced Him always as the Creator of all things. For that reason the Platonic idea of the eternity of matter was rejected, since it would involve an assumption that God was not the Creator of all things.

It has to be understood, however, that by 'God the Father' was often meant the Supreme Being who was source and author of all things, without the thought of relationship within a trinity of persons coming into view. As the name of the living God, the name Father did not rule out the doctrine of a trinity of Persons. It was along this line that Paul argued with the men of Athens, contenting himself with the truths of natural religion, the unity and spirituality of God, His universal moral government and the future life and judgment to come. Similarly it was the one Supreme Being, holy, just and good, that the early Christians presented as the great bulwark against polytheism. Yet even before the books of the New Testament had been collected, the Church's Rule of Faith — the summing up of the Church's faith derived from apostolic preaching and teaching — and the Baptismal Formula in current use, bore testimony to Father, Son, and Holy Ghost. When the Gospel by John came into circulation in the Christian communities, as it did at an early date, its teaching on the Father, the Son, and the Holy Spirit was entering into the thought of the Church.

The problem for Christian theology, however, was how to integrate this teaching intellectually with the faith in the one God. That this was held in the immediacy of faith there can be no doubt. From the earliest extant records it is clear that the Church's doctrine taught that God made Himself known in the Person of Messiah Jesus, and that He had poured His Holy Spirit upon the Church. While no steps were taken in the earliest age of the Church to work these elements into a coherent doctrine of God as Trinity, there is the fact that when the doctrine of the Trinity in Unity came to be formulated, it was immediately accepted as an expression of what had been the faith of the Church from the beginning. One thing is clear, that the doctrine of the Trinity was not arrived at as a result of philosophic reasoning, but was due entirely to meditation on the facts of revelation given in the Scriptures of both the Old Testament and the New, and more especially on the facts concerning the Person of Christ, and God's relation to the world of men through His Spirit. It was indeed the denial of the doctrine through the rise of Gnosticism that shook the Church from its slumbers and compelled it to rethink and restate its dogma.

BEFORE TERTULLIAN: THE LOGOS DOCTRINE

It is to the subtlety of the Greek mind that we owe the first attempt to give intellectual expression to faith in the Trinity. This was connected with the Logos doctrine so much in vogue at the time, not only in the Greek philosophic schools, but in Hebrew and Judaistic culture. It was pressed into service by the Christian apologists to bridge the gulf between a transcendent God and the world of time and place. Since God could not Himself enter into relationship with the world, He chose to send One derived from Himself who could establish that relation. The Christian apologists identified this Logos with Christ, and used it to mark the distinction between the Father and the Son. Thus Christ as the pre-existent One was present from eternity as the Father's thought, finding expression in creation and revelation.

Two facts fundamental to the faith were thus emphasized, that Christ was with the Father before time, and that He was manifested in time when He entered the world. It was assumed that the Logos as the divine rationality had been operating in mankind before Christ came in the flesh, and that, therefore, men possessed fragments of the truth before Christ came. But though the Logos was conceived of as the Father's intelligence or thought, He was also thought of as 'numerically distinct' from the Father, particularly in His functions as Creator, Revealer, and Redeemer. This they supported by Old Testament references. It is clear that they recognized personal distinctions within the Godhead and that, consistently with their monotheism, they insisted that the Father and the Son formed a unity.

With their preoccupation, in the first instance, with the relation of Jesus Christ to the Godhead, they gave less thought to the problem of how the Holy Spirit was related to Deity. Yet, finding the three Persons in the Rule of Faith and the Baptismal Formula, they were not hesitant in proclaiming the Holy Spirit as the One who inspired the prophets and came on the Church at Pentecost. But though the operation of the Spirit was part of the apostolic tradition, His deity and personality were not clearly understood. Theophilus (d. *c.* 186) was the first to speak of a 'triad' in God, and Athenagoras (*c.* 178) speaks of God in three Persons, Father, Son, and Holy Ghost, as the object of Christian worship and adoration. Ignatius uses a picturesque simile in which he compares the faithful to stones forming the Temple, built by God the Father, the cross of Christ being the crane by which the stones were hoisted up, and the Holy Spirit being the hawser! Crude as the figure is, it serves to illustrate the distinction of the three Persons both as to identity and operation.

Thus the lineaments of a trinitarian doctrine were discernible in the early Greek apologists, but it was left to a theologian of the Latin Church to give to the doctrine of the Trinity classic expression which, in its fundamentals, remains to this day the expression of the Church's Trinitarianism—Tertullian (*c.* 160-240).

TERTULLIAN

When Tertullian appeared in the last decade of the second century as the leader and apologist of the African Church, he was faced with a formidable situation in which the Church was torn from within by apostasies, heresies and schisms. He brought great gifts, profound learning, and an ardent disposition to the task confronting him.

In his teaching on the Trinity, Tertullian does not conceal his difficulty in getting a fair hearing for his doctrine, since Christians in general were still impatient of anything that seemed to them to imperil the doctrine of the one only true God. It is significant, however, that Tertullian wrote as one who was upholding not a new doctrine, but the traditional faith of the Church, albeit a faith that was as yet only imperfectly understood or formulated. It was through Tertullian that the elements of the doctrine first found some sort of scientific adjustment and it can be affirmed that no-one before Tertullian, and few besides Tertullian, succeeded in giving anything like a formulated expression to this Trinitarianism.

Tertullian reasserted the distinctions of the three Persons, but he met with the greatest difficulty when he sought to carry these distinctions back into the Godhead without imperilling the unity of God. While he kept his discussion within the framework of the Logos doctrine, the substance of his thinking was derived from the Scriptures and the Rule of Faith. He stated with a definiteness and clarity not known before the full doctrine of the Trinity, asserting a real distinction of Persons which belongs to the substance of the Divine Essence and is not merely derived from the Father, as the Logos theologians held. From the Scriptures and the Rule of Faith he derived the doctrine of the Holy Spirit, to whom he accords absolute deity and eternal distinctness of personality. While the three Persons are one, they are ' one but not identical ', and though they are distinct they are one God and not to be separated. As the trunk and the branch, the fountain and the river, the sun and the sunbeam, cannot be separated, so also the Father and the Son cannot be separated.

Out of the Latin tongue — cumbersome as it is, compared with the Greek — Tertullian forged the concepts that are still used to express the Trinitarian dogma. To him belongs the distinction of first using the words ' Person ', ' Substance ' and ' Trinity ' as applied to Godhead. 'Person' refers to the distinctions within the life of the Godhead, and while it falls short of what is intended and can, to our thought, be misleading as indicating separate independent existence, a better word has not been found. 'Trinity' has the advantage of combining the terms 'tri' and 'unity', thus drawing attention to the Unity of the Tri-Personal God. We also owe to Tertullian the word 'generation' as indicating the relationship of the Son to the Father, a word that is also capable of misapplication, though, here again, a better has not been found. It signifies an eternal relationship between Father and Son which can have no analogy in human relationships.

AFTER TERTULLIAN

After Tertullian, the development of the doctrine passed again to the Greek theologians, and especially to the famous Catechetical School of Alexandria, second only to Athens in intellectual brilliance. It was a distinguishing feature of this School that it adopted a tolerant and genial attitude to heathen culture, and sought to assimilate into the Christian doctrine all that was good in Greek philosophy. Nevertheless, even when in its thought it tended to be speculative and spiritualizing, it sought to be faithful to the distinctive Christian revelation. Origen (*c*. 184-254) was one of the outstanding masters of the Alexandria School and his *First Principles* is the earliest attempt at a system of theology that has come down to us. His special contribution to the doctrine of the Trinity is that he asserted the *eternal* generation of the Son, and sought to expound it as a timeless origination from the Father's essence, which the term 'Son' fails to connote. Origen also put forward the valuable thought that the Trinity is a living Fellowship of Persons, involving an ever-active life in the Godhead, instinct with movement and vitality. In that living process the Son is eternally generated by the Father, and the Spirit eternally proceeds from the Father and the Son. There is, therefore, nothing static, far less stagnant, about the life of God. It is within its own being a state of constant revelation, constant self-giving, and constant responsiveness. This is what C. S. Lewis in recent days sought to express, when he affirmed, somewhat audaciously, 'The life of God is a dance.'

THE NICENE DOCTRINE

The doctrine of the Trinity as affirmed by the Council of Nicea (AD 325) was substantially that formulated by Tertullian and Origen, though its fuller statement removed from Origen's doctrine any doubt there may have been latent in it regarding the deity of Christ being less than that of the Father. Nicea maintained the personal distinctions in the Being of God, and from then on the difficulty was not to establish the Trinity, but to maintain the Unity of the Godhead. The doctrine received fuller attention at the hands of Athanasius and Augustine, Athanasius emphasizing the 'consubstantiality' of the three Persons, that is, the sameness of essence, and Augustine, who had devoted fifteen books to the subject, placing greater emphasis on the absolute Unity of the three Persons than had ever been done before. That the mystery of a Trinity in Unity remained, Augustine freely admits in the typically Augustinian observation: 'We use these terms, not that we may express it, but that it may not remain altogether unexpressed.' After Augustine, no new elements of importance were added to the doctrine accepted by the Church, until it received its fullest and final exposition at the hands of John Calvin.

The seventeenth and eighteenth centuries saw many philosophical constructions of the Trinity, in which the theological elements were rejected, and for them substituted such trinal elements as three modes of manifestation (Theosophy), or three qualities (Kant), or three potencies or energies (Hegel) in a unipersonal God. None of these can be accepted as in accord with the trinitarian teaching of our Lord and with the apostolic revelation given in the Scriptures, which is that of a Trinity in Unity.

From the theoretical aspect the doctrine will remain immersed in mystery, but in the experience of redemption it becomes instinct with life in the love of the Father, the grace of the Son, and the communion of the Spirit.

BOOKS FOR FURTHER STUDY

B. B. Warfield, *Studies in Tertullian and Augustine* (O.U.P., New York, 1931).

J. R. Illingworth, *The Doctrine of the Trinity* (Macmillan, 1907).

CHAPTER II

ATHANASIUS AND THE PERSON OF CHRIST

NO sooner had the doctrine of God as Trinity in Unity been formulated and received general acceptance in the Church, than the question arose as to the place of Jesus of Nazareth, the historical Christ, in this Trinity.

The impact that the historical Jesus had made upon His followers found expression in the confession of Peter at Caesarea Philippi: 'Thou art the Christ, the Son of the living God.' It became the distinctive conviction of the early Church that Jesus was divine, and early records suggest that the most primitive confession of the faith had been 'Jesus is Lord', a confession that undoubtedly raised Jesus of Nazareth to the level of divine sovereignty. Pliny tells us that the Bithynian Christians confessed to him that they were in the habit of meeting together before dawn and saying a hymn 'to Christ as God', and one of the earliest Christian writers, known by the designation '2 Clement', urges his readers to 'think of Jesus as of God, as the judge of the living and the dead', and as 'the one through whom we have known the Father of truth'.

It is thus clear that it was the deity of Christ that had made the first impact upon the mind of the early Church, and this belief has never at any time been absent from the thought of the Church. And by the deity of Christ was understood especially His pre-existence before He entered the world. We find it stated again and again that it was He who had co-operated with the Father in creation, that it was He who conversed with Moses, and that it was He who before the incarnation mediated the knowledge of God to men. He is recognized as 'Lord of the entire cosmos', and Clement of Rome calls Him 'the sceptre of the majesty of God', that is, the one through whom God exercises His sovereignty. He also calls Him 'the High Priest of our offering', and through Him 'we gaze up to the height of heaven'. Ignatius, Bishop of Antioch (martyred 116), describes Christ as 'God incarnate' and 'God manifest as man' and asserts that He 'was in the Spirit united with the Father'.

So insistent was the early Church on the deity of Christ that the other side of His nature tended to be neglected and there arose, even while the apostles were still living, those who denied a human nature to our Lord, holding that His humanity was unreal, a mere shadow or phantasy. From there it was easy to go on and declare that His sufferings were unreal. John had this error in view in his Epistle when he declared that '. . . our hands have handled, of the Word of life' (1 John 1: 1). The sect known as the Docetics, denying that the incarnation was in any sense real, or that the Son had taken to Himself our humanity, or had the capacity to suffer, went so far as to assert that another person had been crucified in Jesus' stead. Hence John's oft-repeated assertion that Christ had come in the flesh, and that the Jesus who had dwelt among men and had been crucified was indeed the Christ.

THE LOGOS CHRISTOLOGY

We had reason to notice in our discussion of the doctrine of the Trinity that it was the apologists who first had to frame an intellectually satisfying explanation of the relation of Christ to God the Father. This they did by means of the Logos doctrine, largely derived from Greek philosophic thought. Because of their conception of the transcendence of God and, to some extent, of the evil of matter, it became necessary to postulate one whom God could send forth to execute His will in creation, and to establish and maintain His relations with the world. This being, derived from God, but subordinate to Him, was identified with Christ. It thus set forth Christ as pre-existent as the Father's thought or mind or reason, and in such acts as creation and revelation we have the expression or going forth of the Logos. Apart from the incarnation and prior to it, the function of the Logos was to be the Father's agent in creating and ordering the universe and revealing truth to men. The Logos was also recognized as the author of reason in man, 'the light that lighteth every man that cometh into the world'. Thus, even before the incarnation, the Logos went forth as an offspring from the Father, as a ray of light from the sun, or a stream from the fountain. This entailed, whatever else it was thought to connote, His oneness with the Father, even when it was the Father's will to send Him forth.

The Christian apologists were careful to distinguish this from the beliefs of pagan mythology regarding the offspring of the gods. 'He is not His Son', says one of the early writers, 'in the sense in which poets and romancers relate the birth of sons to gods, but rather in the sense in which the truth speaks of the Word as eternally in God's bosom. For before anything came into being, He had been His counsellor, His own intelligence and thought. But when God willed to create what He had planned, He engendered and brought forth the Word, the first-begotten of all creation.' While this does not attribute an eternal generation to the Son as son, it does attribute to Him existence with God from eternity, even if His relationship as Son would seem to have begun at the incarnation, or, at any rate, to have had a beginning.

In the incarnation the Logos assumed visible form and became man in Jesus Christ. On the whole, however, the apologists showed little interest in the earthly life of Christ or in His humanity. When His manhood came to view, it was to show that only in suffering could He become a Saviour. Since it was widely held that God could not suffer, it was necessary that if suffering was to be attributed to Christ, it must refer only to His human nature. This emancipation from suffering was typically Greek and was taken over in later times by those who held the doctrine of the impassibility of God.

THE PROBLEM OF THE ONE PERSON

The real problem of the Person of Christ had yet to be faced. It concerned His true deity and true humanity and the relation of the two natures in the Person. The doctrine of the Church as regards the Person was traditionally expressed in three plain propositions: He is perfect Man; He is true God; He is one Christ. In themselves the terms are plain and simple enough, since they affirm the deity of Christ, His manhood, the conjunction of both, and the distinction of the one from the other, but they raised problems of interpretation with which the acutest minds in the Church wrestled in every age. Particularly they raise the problem of the one Person, and how two natures remaining distinct, and each retaining its own proper qualities, could dwell in one person without involving either a dual or a split personality.

ARIANISM

The controversy around this citadel of the faith, which was the longest and fiercest in the history of the Church, was sparked off by the flaring up of the heresy known as Arianism. As early as 318, Arius, a presbyter of the Church in the district of Alexandria, began to make known his conclusions about the Person of Christ. He held that since God is unique, transcendent, and invisible, the being or essence of the Godhead cannot be shared or communicated. For God to impart His substance to some other being, however exalted, would imply that He is divisible and subject to change, which is inconceivable. He concluded, therefore, that what now exists must have come into existence, not by any communication of God's being, but by an act of creation on God's part. From this reasoning four propositions emerged and Arius used all the force of logic to give them point.

1. Christ the Word must be a creature whom God the Father has made out of nothing.
2. As a creature Christ the Word must have had a beginning: 'there was when He was not.'
3. The Son, therefore, can have no communion with or direct knowledge of the Father. Being a creature, and of a different order of existence, He cannot comprehend infinite God.
4. The Son must therefore be liable to change and to sin.

The outcome of this teaching most clearly was to reduce Christ the Word to the status of a demi-god. Even if He is reckoned above all creatures He is still no more than a creature in relation to God. This in effect brought the Christian faith to the very brink of polytheism, and rocked the Church to its very foundations. In 324 the Emperor Constantine turned his attention to the affair, and called an ecumenical council to meet at Nicea in 325.

NICEA

Opposed to Arius was the 'royal hearted' Athanasius (*c.* 296-373), the little deacon from Alexandria with the open vision and the beautiful countenance, as the earliest writers depict him. It is claimed that he possessed 'invincible courage, high business faculty, a singular and piercing knowledge of human nature, a humorous and kindly outlook upon the affairs of men, warm sympathy and magnanimity ', a combination of virtues and graces to which any addition would be superfluous! That he gave long and careful thought to this doctrine of the faith that is for ever associated with his name, is evidenced by the fact that he wrote in his youth a treatise on *The Incarnation of the Word*. Thus when the storm broke, he was prepared to seize the salient points and to direct the controversy. History, secular and ecclesiastical, delights to record that the battle raged around two words, *homoousia* and *homoiousia* applied to the divine nature of our Lord. *Homoousia* signified that He was of the *same* nature as God, while *homoiousia* asserted that He was of *similar* nature to God. The two words scarcely differ as to sound or sight, but a chasm stretches between them as vast as between finitude and infinity. Long before Gibbon, the gibe was current that Athanasius had imperilled the peace of the Church for the sake of a diphthong. But Thomas Carlyle was more discerning when he commented that only an iota separated the two words, yet it marked the difference between paganism and Christianity. This Athanasius clearly discerned. It was the difference that made Christ either creature or Creator. And so the little deacon from Alexandria entered the lists, declaring ' Our contest is for our all '.

There emerged from the Council the Creed that bears its name, which enshrines, by affirmation rather than by definition, the Person of Christ in these memorable words:

> ' I believe . . . in one Lord Jesus Christ, the Son of God, begotten of the Father, God of God, Light of light, very God of very God, begotten not made, co-essential with the Father, by whom all things were made, both in heaven and in earth, who for us men and for our salvation came down and was incarnate, and was made man. He suffered and the third day He rose again, ascended into Heaven, from whence He shall come to judge the quick and the dead.'

AFTER NICEA

For a full century after Nicea, the doctrine of the Two Natures continued to be assailed, first the human side, and then the divine. The Second Ecumenical Council of Constantinople in 382 asserted the integrity of our Lord's human nature, and the Third Ecumenical Council of Ephesus in 428 affirmed the unity of His Person, while the Fourth Ecumenical Council at Chalcedon in 451 gave the fullest expression to the faith of the Church, stating that the Lord Jesus was ' complete as to His Godhead and complete as to His Manhood '.

Subsequent discussion added but little to the defensive, even if not definitive, statement of Chalcedon. The Reformation creeds and confessions made little change in the doctrine of Nicea and Chalcedon as regards the Person of Christ, their concern being rather to make the divine-human Person the object of saving faith and alone the source of salvation. But it can, at least, be claimed that they established more firmly than ever the doctrine of the Incarnate Person in the perfect and unfathomable union of the Two Natures as the all-sufficient Object of faith.

THE MYSTERY OF THE THEANTHROPIC PERSON

The mystery of how the two natures of our Lord were united in one Person, the Nicean and Chalcedon Creeds left unexplained. Even when the full manhood and the true deity had received formal expression, the problem of bringing the two modes of His self-manifestation into the unity of a person was unsolved. It was evident from the beginning that the truth must lie between two unacceptable tendencies, to break up the Person into two, or to mingle the natures so that neither was truly human or truly divine. Athanasius' memorable phrase, which was accepted then and has done service ever since, ' He became what He was not; He continued to be what He was ', is a terse affirmation, but not an explanation.

The very insistence on the complete humanity of Christ and His true deity has had the result of engendering doubt as to whether intercommunion between the two natures could be conceived as possible. The alternatives would seem to be to exalt the human nature to a level that would separate it from the rest of humanity (as is done today by calling it the nature of unfallen Adam), for which there is no evidence in the Gospel records of His earthly life, or to water down His deity by a definition of the incarnation as involving a kenosis or self-emptying (for which the passage and the word in Philippians 2: 7 give no support), so that our Lord on earth was subject to all human limitation, with the possible exception of sin.

The factor that is forgotten, and may well be the only key to the problem, is the ministry of the Holy Spirit in the Person and life of Christ. That Spirit, who had prepared His humanity and kept the unborn Child free from the taint of His mother's sin, never left Him, but throughout all the temptations and sufferings of His life and death brought to His human soul the light and comfort and strength which He needed to accomplish His task. In the light of that gracious ministry we can understand, in some measure, how the divine nature was acting under human conditions, and how the human nature was acting in fullest unity with the divine. That Spirit, who shared the eternal counsels of the Godhead, unified the consciousness of Christ so that there could be no possibility of division or dualism within Him. For this reason we can understand how there was nothing unnatural or unhuman about the self-consciousness of Jesus even when He was in unbroken communion with the supernatural and eternal.

However we explain it — and a full knowledge must pass our comprehension — saving faith has always reached out to One who is perfect Man, true God, and one Christ, and in the strength and fellowship of this faith we as Christians are called to abide.

BOOKS FOR FURTHER STUDY

D. M. McIntyre, *Christ the Lord* (Marshall, Morgan and Scott, 1922).

B. B. Warfield, *The Person and Work of Christ*. Edited by S. G. Craig (Presbyterian and Reformed Publishing Co., 1950).

CHAPTER III

AUGUSTINE AND THE DOCTRINE OF MAN

SINCE the Christian faith has always insisted that man can properly be studied only in his relation to God, it was both logical and natural that attention should have been focused on the doctrine of man only after the doctrine of God and of the God-Man had been studied. Not that reflection on man's nature, origin and destiny had at any time been absent from the thought of the Church, but other and more urgent problems pressed the doctrine of man to the periphery of Christian thought. It was in the fourth and fifth centuries that the Church turned its attention to a study of human nature, and its theology passed from its principal domain, that of God, to the study of man in sin and grace. That this doctrine was now ready to be discussed is evidenced by the fact that there appeared simultaneously two men who represented the opposite poles of doctrine, Pelagius and Augustine. With these two theologians, theology passed from East to West, and from the region of theology proper to that of anthropology. It can be said that the discussion of this doctrine was more congenial to Western thought, which was less subtle and speculative than the trend in the Eastern schools.

THE DOCTRINE IN EASTERN THEOLOGY

It is not altogether a fact that the doctrine of man gave no scope for the rather subtle speculation to which the Greek mind was so partial. The nature of man as soul and body, or as Plato held, body, soul and spirit, the origin of the soul and its immortality, the fact of sin, and the ever-present fact of death, occupied the minds of Eastern theologians for many generations. Athanasius indulged in his favourite metaphysics and mysticism in discussing man's primeval state, the entrance of sin and its devastations in human nature and effects in destiny. How sin passed into the race and the extent to which it left man free to exercise his will were matters of continual theological discussion. This raised also the question of what was meant by the image of God in man, and the extent to which that image was defaced by sin. There was general agreement that man had been created perfect, a state that involved sinlessness and communion with God, and that his present state of sin was due to his disobedience. It can be said, however, that the Greek Fathers took, on the whole, a more optimistic view of man and were less prone to dwell on his general depravity than the theologians of the West. To them sin was more a wound inflicted on man's nature than a state of moral corruption and spiritual death. They were agreed on three points: that man was created in moral perfection; that all the race shared in Adam's sin through the exercise of free will which is an inalienable possession of man, so that sin was transmitted, through heredity or recapitulation, to all the members of the race; and that the grace of God was needed to restore human nature to its lost purity. In their struggle with Gnostic fatalism, they felt the need to conserve human freedom and they, therefore, laid greater emphasis on the freedom of the will than the theologians of the West.

THE DOCTRINE IN THE WEST

Similar views of man were held in the West, with the main emphasis on the two facts of man's fallen state and consequent need of grace, and his possession of free will to the extent of involving personal responsibility. But it was left to Pelagius, a monk of British birth, to propound a doctrine of man that compelled the Church to rethink the whole position and formulate its doctrine with something of the clarity and care given to the doctrines of the Trinity and the Person of Christ. The man to do this was Augustine. What Arius was to Athanasius, Pelagius was to Augustine, the antagonist who forced a statement and clarification of the issue.

Pelagius, described as ' a fashionable teacher at Rome ', was, it is said, of blameless character and correct living. He was shocked at the injustice done to human nature by this doctrine of depravity which the Church taught and he did not hesitate to condemn it as an insult to man's Creator. He put forward three propositions that were diametrically opposed to catholic belief. The first was that all men could be sinless if they chose, and that certain men had in fact lived in complete freedom from sin. From that he went on to argue that if man can live free from sin, then he can come into the world free from sin, thus denying the presupposition of original sin. On this principle he concluded that man had no need of supernatural assistance in the way of grace to enable him to live a righteous life. It was this denial of the need and the reality of grace that roused the Church to defend what it regarded as a central doctrine of its faith.

In open opposition to Pelagius, Augustine, the Bishop of Hippo, took the field and set out to establish the doctrine of sin and grace that is for ever associated with his name. Augustine (354-430), the most noted of the Latin Fathers, has been assigned a commanding place as ' incomparably the greatest figure between Paul the Apostle and Luther the Reformer that the Christian Church has ever possessed ', and after a millennium and a half his influence is still a living force in the Church of God. To Augustine the struggle with Pelagianism was a struggle for the very foundations of Christianity. In the assertion of the freedom of man's will and the denial of the need of divine grace, Pelagius raised the issue whether, since man by his power could attain to eternal felicity, there was any need for Christianity at all. In his controversy with Pelagius Augustine has given to the Church the doctrine of man that, with some modifications, is still the faith of the Church catholic. His doctrine had several distinct features which, if not entirely new insights, gave clearer expression than ever before to the faith of the Church. The anthropology of Augustine centres round three main points: the original state of man, the nature and consequences of man's first sin, and the power of divine grace to restore human nature. These three are, of course, inter-related in any discussion of man, for man's original image and primitive state have a direct bearing on the measure of his loss caused by the Fall, and the consequent necessity and nature of grace.

MAN'S RELATION TO GOD

Augustine's starting-point was that in formulating a doctrine of man, God and the human soul must always be viewed in relation to each other. To him the soul was made for God and in its unfallen state was never meant to subsist apart from Him. Even as a sinless being man could realize his destiny only through a habitual dependence on the grace of God by which God was continually imparting Himself. The soul's relationship to God, as he liked to put it, was that of a receptive vessel to which God was imparting His life and light and strength. In this fellowship man had his true freedom which consisted in, not inability to sin, but ability not to sin (not *non posse peccare*, but *posse non peccare*). This potential righteousness which was given to man constituted a potential immortality.

Augustine was not deeply interested in the Greek debate as to whether man was tripartite (body, soul and spirit as distinct entities) or bipartite (body and soul, or material and spiritual). He used the expression 'body, soul, and spirit', as Paul does on one occasion, but he groups soul and spirit as a unity over against the body. In this unity the will is the central faculty and characteristic feature. This emphasis on the will and its impulse towards self-realization is the new feature in the psychology of Augustine. This is more in accord with biblical usage, which does not regard the terms used — variously spirit, soul, flesh, heart — as parts or divisions of man, but rather as media through which the man expresses himself. It is in this sense that Augustine generally uses 'will'.

THE NATURE AND CONSEQUENCES OF SIN

The fact that man was under probation implied that he could sin and so lose the fellowship of God. This actually happened when Adam yielded to self-love, the essence of all sin. Here Augustine emphasized the voluntary nature of sin, placing it not on a natural but on a moral and ethical basis. As man's life consisted in communion with God, so his sin caused his life to be cut from its source of being and sustenence in God. In this way man was brought under the dominion of an evil necessity: man can no longer realize his destiny or will the true good.

Since to Augustine the essence of sin lay in its defection from God, the supreme good and source of life, it was natural to regard sin as a privation, not an addition to life but a subtraction from it. He uses the illustration of a plant in which the cessation of life means decay. To us, with modern ideas of bacteriology, decay is not just the mere absence of life, it is the presence of the agents of disintegration in the form of bacteria which take over the breaking down of organized matter. So Augustine's doctrine that evil is merely the privation of good, and has no metaphysical reality, is open to the serious objection that it deals only with the metaphysical aspect of sin, and not with the moral and ethical, and so does not do justice to the positive character of sin in experience.

But tracing sin, not to the solicitations of sense, but to self-love Augustine is on surer ground when he teaches that it is through an inward fall, in which man substituted the love of self for the love of God, that the solicitations of sense have power over our lives. In abandoning God, the soul became abandoned by God, and the inner harmony of human nature was lost. This prepared the way for man's subjection to concupiscence, or the solicitations of sense, as shown in the sense of shame that immediately entered the consciousness of our first parents.

THE TRANSMISSION OF SIN

It is quite obvious that Augustine is not clear or consistent in his view on the transmission of sin. Sometimes he speaks as if sin had been transmitted by a mysterious unity of the race, implying that we were all present in the individual Adam so that the whole race was the one man that sinned. Sometimes he speaks of it more in the sense of modern realists as if Adam's sin corrupted the very fabric of our nature, and the corrupt nature corrupts those to whom it is communicated. At other times, he is content to explain it in terms of mere heredity. But throughout he is insistent that Adam transmitted both the guilt and the corruption belonging to it to his posterity. It took the theologians of the post-Reformation period to explain the transmission of sin in terms of the federal or covenant relationship in which Adam stood to God on behalf of the race, so that when the head of the covenant fell, he dragged the race with him. This idea is central to Covenant Theology as a whole, since its basic principle is that since man was ruined through a representative, man can be restored through a representative.

Augustine has no illusion, however, about the damage done to our nature by sin. As he took the high view of man's original state, so he took the dark view of his fallen state. While he recognizes that the soul has not lost all the sense of its primal relation to God, nor ceases to sigh after Him, he asserts that man has no longer the power to realize the true end of his being, but that through ignorance and evil habit he sinks constantly deeper into bondage. To Augustine, as indeed to us, 'total depravity' meant that sin affected man in the totality of his nature so that no element or faculty can be eliminated from his fallen condition.

Nowhere, Augustine holds, can the damage done to man's nature by sin be seen more clearly than in the sphere of man's will. While God had endowed man with free will, Adam used his will for sinning, and so the faculty of will is impaired. Will as a mere faculty he distinguished from the willingness that is the product and expression of our entire nature. The faculty of will he regards as morally neutral, responsive to the inclinations and behests of the nature, a mere weathercock, as he puts it, ready to be turned in any direction by the breeze that blows from the heart. But since the Fall has diseased and perverted man's nature, his will must act in the direction indicated by his nature. This entails that the will of man is enslaved by an evil nature; a corrupt nature makes a corrupt use of its will. What has become, therefore, of man's free will? It is still free, replies Augustine, to carry out the wishes of the nature, but since the nature is corrupt man's will is free only to do evil. Man lost his *posse non peccare*, his freedom not to sin. Thus man's free will avails for sinning, but it does not avail for good unless and until the nature is changed and the will is freed by God's grace.

Augustine is not, however, a physical or metaphysical determinist in the sense in which he is sometimes thought to be. He recognizes that psychologically man is free within the limit of his capacity and is the efficient cause of the evil done by him. Though man has a free choice he opts for a perverse course. It is in this sense that Augustine uses the phrase: 'the will is free, but not freed.' Man's loss of freedom is rooted in his moral character.

It is doubtful if in all this Augustine does full justice to man's will as a faculty that can act either in harmony with or in opposition to the nature. It can disobey the dictates of the heart, even in unregenerate man. What lacked due emphasis in his teaching is that the faculty of will has shared in the general ruin of man's nature (it were strange if it, alone of all his faculties, had escaped) and that the will is not only enslaved but diseased, won over to the side of sin and exercising its willingness in the direction of sinning. In the choice between good and evil, it no longer resists the pressure of the heart towards evil because its own inclination is in that direction.

THE RESTORATION OF DIVINE GRACE

It is in this context of an enslaved will that Augustine introduces his doctrine of grace, the doctrine of all others on which he has shed the greatest light. It is said that Augustine replaced the metaphysical dualism of matter and spirit, so familiar in Greek thought, by the ethical and religious dualism of sin and grace. It would be correct to say that he recognizes in grace the divine response to man's inability. Augustine himself could never lose sight of his indebtedness to the grace of God that lifted his life from the mire of sin and impurity. While grace properly stands for all forms of divine aid, to Augustine it particularly stood for the inner operation of God's Spirit — 'an internal and secret power, wonderful and ineffable' — by which man is made a new creature and kept in a state of salvation. Augustine is fond of representing this grace as in essence the writing of God's law upon our hearts so that it appears thereafter as our own choice and wish. Thus he shows that grace does not damage free will, but acts upon it in setting it free and then acts through it when it is freed. Augustine's conception of the grace of God in renewing the will and restoring it to its true freedom finds terse expression in his prayer: 'Give what Thou commandest, and command what Thou wilt.'

When Augustine comes to discuss the means of grace, especially baptism, his doctrine of grace comes into conflict with his doctrine of the Church, and though he does not bind the conferring of grace to the ordinance of baptism, he does hold that no-one can be saved who has not been baptized. To us the essence of evangelicalism, as against sacerdotalism, is that the soul may have direct access to God without the use of any means, though we recognize that the means are appointed to be channels of grace. In spite of this lapse, Augustine was no sacerdotalist, for no man was more distinctly anti-ecclesiastical in the sense that he made everything that concerned salvation to come from God and depend wholly and only upon God. Indeed, as has been frequently pointed out, his theology of grace, rightly understood, had in it that which destroyed this very conception of the mechanical transmission of grace. It is not too much to say, as B. B. Warfield points out, that if Augustine was not the first of the Reformers, it was to Augustine's theology of grace that we owe the Reformation and the emancipation of man's spirit from the bondage of priestcraft and dependence on human merit. We know that his doctrine of grace was taken hold of by Luther and made the basis of the Reformed theology.

Augustine's contribution to the doctrine of man was not only a great advance on the thought of the Church in earlier ages, and the basis on which the theologians of the sixteenth century were to formulate their doctrine, but in its main features it remains the distinctive doctrine of man to this day. With the coming of the scientific age, man has been discussed in other contexts; in his relation to natural life around him, as in biology; in relation to the laws that govern his natural existence, as in physics; in relation to his social environment, as in sociology; but it has been left to Christian revelation to shed light upon man in his relation to his Maker. This was Augustine's standpoint, and it is still the point of reference of Christian anthropology.

BOOKS FOR FURTHER STUDY

B. B. Warfield, *Studies in Tertullian and Augustine* (O.U.P., New York, 1931).

J. Laidlaw, *The Bible Doctrine of Man* (T. & T. Clark, 1905).

CHAPTER IV

ANSELM AND THE DOCTRINE OF THE ATONEMENT

THERE is in primitive Church theology a slower unfolding of the doctrine of atonement than of any other of the foundation truths of Christianity. The exact nature of the redemption wrought by Christ was not made the subject of close study in the early Church for the two reasons, that the apostolic Church, and the New Testament records, made the significance of Christ's death sufficiently clear for faith to rest on it, and that the early Church was preoccupied with more pressing problems that called for urgent attention and were fundamental to its faith. It were futile to unfold the meaning of the atonement until there had been some understanding and some consensus of opinion on the Person who rendered the atonement. In other words, the doctrine of atonement could not be properly investigated until attention had been given to those doctrines which form its presuppositions.

At no time, however, did Christians lose the consciousness that they were redeemed by the death of Christ; at no time did they lose sight of their indebtedness to His cross. It can also be affirmed that there never was a time when the Church did not attribute a propitiatory efficacy to Christ's death and regard it as the ground of pardon and peace. It could scarcely be otherwise considering the emphasis it receives in the Epistles of Paul and the fullness with which it is treated in the New Testament generally.

But while there is free use of Scripture language, there is little evidence of any deep insight into its meaning. Certainly there is no attempt to build up a theory, or a developed theology, of the atonement.

THE GREEK FATHERS

The Apostolic Fathers (AD 90-140) are profuse in their allusions to redemption through the blood of Christ, but their theology in general is more Johannine than Pauline, and a mystical element enters into their interpretation. For example 1 Clement asks us to 'look stedfastly upon the blood of Christ, and recognize how precious it is to God His Father, because it was shed for our salvation and obtained for all the world the grace of repentance', thus connecting the moral results of Christ's death directly with His sacrifice. He further asserts that 'through the love He had for us Christ our Lord gave His blood for us by the will of God, and His flesh for our flesh, and His soul for our souls'. That Christ 'died for our sins' was by far the most frequent reference to His death. The Epistle to Diognetus (early second century) has a passage of absorbing interest and beauty, which will bear quotation in full:

> 'He Himself took on Him the burden of our iniquities, He gave His Son to be a ransom for us, the Holy One for transgressors, the Blameless One for the wicked, the Righteous One for the unrighteous, the Incorruptible One for the corruptible, the Immortal One for them that are mortal. For what other thing was capable of covering our sin, but His righteousness? By what other one was it possible that we, the wicked and ungodly, should be justified than by the only Son of God? O, sweet exchange! O, unsearchable operation! O, benefits surpassing all expectation, that the wickedness of many should be hid in a single righteous One, and that the righteousness of One should justify many transgressors!'

With Origen there creeps in just a suggestion of what became known afterwards as the 'Ransom to Satan' theory, though Origen himself is quite clear that the sacrifice was offered to God, even though he seems to hold that Satan was outwitted in the transaction. Origen, nevertheless, was the first to show a developed doctrine of the atonement, even if it lacked many of the elements that entered into what became the accepted doctrine of the Church.

With Athanasius we enter a new phase of understanding of the meaning of the death of Christ, inasmuch as personal salvation is at the centre of all Athanasius' theology. Athanasius is the first to bring the incarnation into direct touch with our redemption. To explain the reason for the incarnation he goes back to the original creation of man and to his fall and his passing under the sentence of death. He recognizes that repentance alone would not suffice to stay the hand of justice. It could only be done by the Logos, the very Creator of the world, in whose rational image man was made, taking our nature upon Him that He might redeem us. Athanasius would seem to be the first writer after Paul to develop a doctrine of the death of Christ as a satisfaction to divine justice, while in his thinking the doctrine of a price having been paid to the devil disappears completely. It is true that the Ransom to Satan view did appear later and held sway in the Middle Ages, though much less generally than is commonly asserted. The devil is supposed, through the fall of man, to have acquired certain rights over him which God in justice cannot set aside. When God gives His only-begotten Son for the ransom of the world, Satan is deceived and accepts Christ in lieu of the world of sinners, only to find that he cannot hold Him. But most theologians rejected out of hand this mythological theory, and Gregory of Nazianzus (d. 390) pours scorn on it in these words: ' Now, since a ransom belongs only to him who holds us in bondage, I ask, to whom was this offered and for what cause? If to the Evil One, shame on the outrage! Then the robber receives a ransom, not only for God, but which consists of God Himself, and he receives such an illustrious payment for his tyranny!'

THE LATIN FATHERS

In the West generally, under the influence of the Latin conceptions of law and justice, there developed the idea of Christ's death as a satisfaction to divine justice. This began with Tertullian who is the first theologian to use the terms ' satisfaction ' and ' merit ' in this connection. It is a fact, however, that the writers never lose sight of the truth that it is God's love which is the cause of the reconciliation. They never present it as a case of a wrathful, vengeful God appeased by the sacrifice of His Son, as they are too often misrepresented as doing. Augustine, whose doctrine of grace prepared the way for an understanding of the sacrifice of Christ as the ground of reconciliation, is insistent that it is not a case of being reconciled and then loved, but rather loved and then reconciled. The very sacrifice of the Mass, which in some form or other already had a footing in the middle of the third century, pointed to the death of Christ as a propitiatory sacrifice for sin.

ANSELM OF CANTERBURY

What we notice about all these expressions of faith is that there is no attempt to bring the various aspects of Christ's saving work into a unity. Not until the eleventh century was the nature of the atonement made the subject of investigation at the hands of Anselm of Canterbury (*c.* 1033-1109). Not that Anselm resided much at Canterbury, for after his enthronement as Archbishop, to which he was inflexibly opposed, he hastened back to his monastery in Gaul, and there he went on with his interrupted studies.

It was Anselm who gave reasoned form to the doctrine that Christ made satisfaction for sin and merited salvation for His people. The keynotes of his doctrine are *satisfaction* and *merit*, and while he presses these to an extent that is now recognized as a weakness in his doctrine, his statement became the basis of all succeeding presentation of the Reformed doctrine of atonement. His great work, *Cur Deus Homo?* (' Why did God become Man?'), to which Dr James Denney paid the tribute that it is ' the truest and greatest book on the atonement that has ever been written ' (*The Death of Christ*, p. 188), is first of all significant as indicating the angle from which the atonement was being approached, which was that of the Person of Christ. The particular context in which it was being studied generally at the time was the humiliation of Christ. What was being discussed was the necessity for the Son of God undergoing shame and humiliation in His sufferings and death in order that men might be forgiven. Could not God in His omnipotence have redeemed us as easily as He had created the world? Could He not forgive sin out of His pure mercy without this infinite expenditure of means? Or, if mediation was necessary, why should not an angel be chosen as mediator instead of the only-begotten Son?

These were the questions which Anselm set himself to answer in his epoch-making book. He was the first who, with a complete view of the problem, raised this question in its whole compass and sought to give it a reasoned answer.

Anselm saw at once that if there existed a necessity for the incarnation and death of Christ in order that man might be saved, then this necessity must lie either in the nature of sin, or in the nature of God, or in both. Augustine had already gone deep into the nature of sin, but he had not studied the other side, the question of how the nature of God requires Him to react against sin in the form of condemnation and punishment. Anselm disposes at once of the 'Ransom to Satan' theory and rules it out of court. He deals with sin as something which robs God of His honour. Obedience he regards as a debt which man owes to God, and failure to pay this debt is sin.

That leads him to the second step, that even if men were now able to pay the debt of obedience, that would not make up for the disobedience already given. He now raises the question whether it was possible for God to forgive sins by an act of mercy alone, without satisfaction being made to His injured honour. If God commands men to forgive, why cannot He forgive freely Himself? Anselm answers: because He is not a private person, but God. God's will is not His own in the sense that anything is permissible to Him, or becomes right because He wills it. What God is determines what God does. God cannot deal with sin except as a holy God sees it to be. If it is not punished, or adequate satisfaction made for it, it is unjustly forgiven.

Anselm then goes on to ask, if sin can be forgiven only on condition that a proportional satisfaction be made for it, who then can make this satisfaction? Man from his own resources cannot do it. From this point Anselm goes on to develop the conditions under which a true satisfaction is possible and to show how these conditions are fulfilled in Jesus Christ. Such a satisfaction can be offered only by God Himself, yet it must be offered in human nature, or it would not be a satisfaction for man. Hence the necessity for the Redeemer being both God and Man.

It will be seen why Anselm's theory is known as the Satisfaction Theory of the atonement. Its ethical form is impressive as it insists on the need of satisfaction and on the voluntary nature of Christ's sufferings for the sake of righteousness. But it omits all reference to the penalty of sin in the atonement. At no point does it bring the satisfaction of Christ into direct contact with the punitive will of God. Further he represents the debt of sin as being paid by someone who stands outside the debtor or sinner, and he fails to bring to view the voluntary identification of the Sin-bearer with the sinner, of Christ with those who shelter in Him.

AFTER ANSELM

Peter Abelard (1079-1142) was the first after Anselm to take up the study of the atonement, but his work bears little trace of the influence of Anselm. He occupies, indeed, the opposite pole from Anselm, and is justly regarded as the father of the Moral Influence Theory of the atonement. He rejects every form of the Satisfaction doctrine and places the effects of Christ's sufferings and death wholly in their moral results. The amazing love of God in giving up His Son for us enkindles in us a responsive love which becomes the ground for the forgiveness of our sins. Redemption, he declares, is the greatest love enkindled in us by Christ's passion, a love which not only delivers us from the bondage of sin, but also acquires for us the true freedom of children where love instead of fear becomes the ruling affection.

Bernard (1091-1153), the next writer, rose up at once to attack, and he rejected Abelard's doctrine as entirely out of harmony with the faith of the Church. In reducing Christ's sufferings and death to an example of love, Bernard holds that Abelard robs them of that redemptive significance which the New Testament gives them and which the Church had always taught. Bernard makes a valuable contribution, lacking in Anselm, in that he recognizes the organic relation of Christ and His people as explaining how the satisfaction of one should avail for the many. The atonement is thus not a bare external substitution of the innocent for the guilty, but of the Head for the members of His body. 'There is found no longer', says Bernard, 'one who sinned and one who satisfied, because the one Christ is Head and body.'

Thomas Aquinas (1227-1274) develops this thought of Bernard's, of Christ suffering as Head of the Church, and of the Church as the mystical body of Christ being reckoned along with Christ her Head as one. He also brings to view, what is omitted by Anselm, that the satisfaction of Christ embraced the endurance of the penal consequences of sin which included death itself. This thought was not by any means new, but Aquinas secures it in a clearly defined principle. At the same time he does justice to Christ's love and obedience, and is as emphatic as his predecessors in showing that it is not the atonement that is the spring of God's love to man, but rather that it is the amazing love of God that lies behind the atonement.

Subsequent theologians added little to the doctrine as laid down by Anselm and supplemented by Bernard and Aquinas, and the Reformers took it over as their own, with an added emphasis on the penal aspect of the sufferings that provided the atonement. They were careful to attribute redemptive value, not only to the sufferings and death of Christ, but to the obedience of His life as well. This they did on the ground that men needed, in order to stand before God, not only freedom from God's wrath, but also a righteousness which they could gain only through the fufilment of the law of God. The 'satisfaction' of Christ included this fulfilment of the divine law, and so 'obedience' became the key-word of the Reformed doctrine as embracing the whole of Christ's work. From the Reformation era this doctrine passed into the creeds of the Reformed churches as the standard of orthodox belief. Its distinctive feature is that it places forgiveness of sin and the acceptance of the sinner upon a righteous basis and puts us right with God in presence of His own eternal law. Thus harmony with law and justice has been restored by Christ and the fundamental order of the universe has been vindicated. In this is rooted man's own peace of conscience, as well as the reconciliation into which God invites the sinner.

MODERN OPPOSITION TO THE DOCTRINE

It is true that the modern mind offers considerable opposition to the Satisfaction view of the atonement, which it generally refers to as 'the forensic view'. But it is also true that it offers considerable opposition to any theory of the atonement. Why make a mystery into a theory, an infinite truth into a finite one, we are asked. Why try to reduce the things of God into the narrow limits of our field of vision? It is, we are told, a debasing of the great mystery of the divine love that it should be made subject to analysis; better by far to accept it in all its impenetrable wonder and be duly humbled in its presence! While it is true that much in the atonement is impenetrable to the human mind, there is also much in it on which Scripture has shed revealing light. It is surely a truer spirit of reverence to follow humbly the divine unveiling than to stand blindfold in awe before an impenetrable mystery. In a matter that concerns us as vitally as the foundation of our peace with God, we ought not to be content with a blind venture. Moreover, a way of forgiveness and restoration that failed to satisfy our own moral consciousness could not for long be the foundation of our peace. For that reason we must be convinced that God, from whom we derive our moral consciousness, finds satisfaction, that He is reconciled before He offers His reconciliation to us. And this is precisely what the much derided ' satisfaction ' view of the atonement is calculated to do. It deals with God first, and only secondarily with us, and in a transaction that gives satisfaction to God we find satisfaction. Thus propitiation is the basis of reconciliation. The atonement is more than an at-one-ment. It is first and foremost a putting right of what has gone wrong, and a putting it right where it has gone wrong, and only then can parties come together and there is an at-one-ment.

Thus we can see that in Anselm's Satisfaction Theory the basis of all succeeding study of the atonement had been laid. It ensures the approach to the atonement which we call ' evangelical ', that is, the approach from God's side. It has the merit of setting the doctrine in its true relation to the attributes of God and the realities of man's guilt.

BOOKS FOR FURTHER STUDY

R. S. Franks, *The Work of Christ* (Nelson, 1962).
J. K. Mozley, *The Doctrine of the Atonement* (Duckworth, 6th ed., 1947).

CHAPTER V

LUTHER AND THE DOCTRINE OF JUSTIFICATION BY FAITH ALONE

WE have already observed an organic growth in theological development from root to fruit. The nature of the Godhead with whom we have to do, the suitableness of the Person through whom we have access to God, the reality of the sin that makes it necessary for us to deal with God, and the divine provision by which sin can be put away, are all matters of prime concern to every reasoning soul, but how to translate this faith into a vital personal experience has still to be considered. And this is the aspect of the faith on which the fullest light was cast in the era associated with the Reformation. Without doubt the divine principle on which the salvation of Christ is made over to the sinner and enters his consciousness is justification, the doctrine above all others associated with the Reformation.

Here, as elsewhere, we must recognize that Christians right down through the early ages of the Church discerned this principle and acted on it. The fact of acceptance with God on the merits of Christ and by grace alone was never absent from the belief of the Church. Even when there is no explicit reference to justification by faith, there is an outright rejection of justification by works.

THE EARLY FATHERS

Though specific references to the doctrine are admittedly sparse in the early Fathers, there are occasions when it is clearly and forcibly expressed, either as a confession of faith or an utterance of experience. For example, Clement of Rome, who may have been Paul's fellow-labourer, has this very full statement: 'All the ancient Fathers descended from Abraham, both before the Law and after the Law, were glorified and magnified, not through themselves, nor through their works of righteousness which they had done, but through His will. Therefore, we also, being called through His will in Christ Jesus, are not justified through ourselves, neither through our own wisdom or understanding or purity or works which we have done in holiness of heart, but through faith, that faith through which the Almighty God has justified all who ever lived.'

His namesake, Clement of Alexandria, who presided over the Catechetical School before Origen, had imbibed many of the principles of the Neo-Platonic philosophy and was very defective in his teaching on free will; he was nevertheless very clear on the nature and standing of faith. He insists that faith is not natural or the product of man's unaided effort, but the operation of the Spirit of God. Tertullian, who was the first to apply the term 'satisfaction' to man's good deeds by way of securing the favour of God, is quite clear on the ground of a sinner's acceptance. To Athanasius acceptance by faith in Christ was the substance of the gospel, as it was also to Anselm and Bernard. To Augustine it was part and parcel of his understanding of grace.

CAUSE OF DECLENSION

Though there were outstanding examples of adherence to the New Testament doctrine of justification, as we have shown, it is sad to reflect that on the whole the Church went astray on this vital matter earlier than perhaps on any other tenet of the faith. This was undoubtedly due to the place it gave to the sacraments as mechanical means of salvation. When regeneration and forgiveness became associated with the rite of baptism, it is evident that there could be no clear or strong light on the doctrine of justification by faith alone. When the term 'justification' was used, it did service to cover all that was involved in the supposed effects of baptism, regeneration, quickening, forgiveness and renewal. In particular, justification became confused with sanctification as something to be infused into the sinner, as making a person just rather than as declaring him just. It was widely taught that sin committed after baptism, and so not washed away in the waters of baptism, had to be got rid of in some other way, and this belief opened the door to many of the abuses practised by the Church in the Middle Ages, penance, confession, priestly absolution in this life, and purgatory in the life to come. In short, the application of salvation became more a mechanical affair, manipulated by the priesthood and reached in no other way. That there were many in the Roman Church who repudiated this cumbersome machinery of salvation is not to be denied. Luther found many of these in the religious orders of his day and he says of them: 'Wherefore, they finding in themselves no good works to set against the wrath and judgment of God, did flee to the death and passion of Christ, and were saved in this simplicity.' There can be no doubt but that the clear light cast upon the nature of the atonement by Anselm and Bernard had its effect on the catholic doctrine of acceptance with God. The clearer it became that Christ had made satisfaction for the sins of men which was of infinite value with God, the more absurd it appeared to add to this the satisfaction of men. This may explain why at the opening of the sixteenth century the new truth dawned on several men independently of each other, in France, in Switzerland, in Germany and in Britain.

THE DOCTRINE IN THE NINETY-FIVE THESES

It stands true, nevertheless, that it was the doctrine of justification by faith alone, and all it implies in a sinner's approach to God, that marked the cleavage between the Reformation era and the ages that went before. The Reformers themselves were conscious of this, as were also their Roman Catholic opponents. The cardinal before whom Luther was examined put his finger on two propositions out of the Ninety-five Theses which he asked the Reformer absolutely to recant. They were, first, the assertion (in the 58th thesis) that the merits of Christ alone work effectively without the intervention of the pope and therefore cannot be drawn upon by indulgences, and, second, the assertion that the sacraments do not work effectively unless received by faith. There Luther had attacked two tenets fundamental to the Roman system of salvation. In these two assertions of his are embodied the essence of evangelicalism, salvation as the immediate gift of Christ, and faith alone as the instrument of reception of the grace of God.

While it is true that justification by faith is not once mentioned by Luther in the Ninety-five Theses, it is also clear that the doctrine underlies them throughout. Luther had already given his exposition of justification in his lectures on Romans of 1515-16, and from that time he had been diligently preaching this doctrine from pulpit and chair and had already converted his immediate community to the evangelical faith. What is marked by the posting of the Theses on the church door of Wittenberg is the issuing of the Reformation out of the narrow confines of the university circles of Wittenberg and its start on its career as a world movement. In that great doctrine, as has been said, Luther set the evangelical principle flatly in opposition to the sacerdotal and cast it into the arena of world-wide conflict. It was this that made the posting of the Theses the first act of Reformation.

LUTHER'S DISCOVERY

Where and how did Luther come at the truth that broke his chains and brought him into the liberty of the gospel? Tradition has it that it was while he was painfully mounting the steps of the Scala Santa in Rome to seek release from purgatory for his grandfather, repeating the Paternoster at each step, that he heard as it were a voice from heaven 'The just shall live by faith'. The tradition may or may not be well founded in historical fact, but there is no gainsaying the fact that it was in 1503 that Luther made what Thomas Carlyle calls his 'most blessed discovery', the discovery of a Latin Bible in the library of his monastery at Erfurt. With a conscience deeply burdened, and a heart yearning for inner satisfaction, Luther read on, and even Paul whom he had shunned before as terrifying in his insistence on righteousness, wrath, and judgment, he now found speaking to his personal state. The Epistles to the Romans and the Galatians he made his constant study. There is no doubt at all but that the whole of Luther's training and experience up to now had put him in a favourable position to study this subject and to appreciate all its revolutionary implications. He had been brought up in a religion that taught justification by human merit, and Luther was behind none in his diligence to secure this justification. He left no stone unturned to learn more of the doctrine of his justification, no effort was spared to attain to this pinnacle of merit that would bring peace to his soul and give him standing as a teacher in his Church. In this respect he started pretty much where Saul the Pharisee had started, and so Luther was the better able to enter into the sweep of Paul's mighty argument in Galatians and Romans. As he had endured travail of soul while under the distorted view of the gospel given to him by his Church, so now he entered into exultant joy and confident assurance as he felt himself emancipated from the chains which had fettered him. And this new-found joy and confidence entered his soul through the exercise of faith, a faith that has no merit except its capacity to receive, and no power except its power to submit and obey. Such a faith left nothing to himself, as he was accustomed to exclaim, ' nothing, absolutely nothing '. Hence the positive terms of his great confession:

> ' I Dr Martin Luther, the unworthy evangelist of the Lord Jesus Christ, thus think and thus affirm: That this article, namely, that faith alone, without works, justifies us before God, can never be overthrown, for Christ alone, the Son of God, died for our sins; but if Christ alone takes away our sins, then men, with all their works, are to be excluded from all concurrence in procuring the pardon of sin and justification. Nor can I embrace Christ otherwise than by faith alone, He cannot be apprehended by works. But if faith, before works follow, apprehend the Redeemer, it is undoubtedly true that faith alone, before works and without works, appropriates the benefits of redemption, which is no other than justification, or deliverance from sin. This is our doctrine; so the Holy Spirit teaches, and the whole Christian Church. In this, by the grace of God, will we stand fast. Amen.'

EFFECTS OF THE DOCTRINE

Now, while the Reformers differed among themselves on many doctrines of the faith, and were not slow to express their differences, it is remarkable that no two opinions existed among them on the doctrine of justification by faith alone. It was as freely accepted by Calvin as by Luther, by Zwingli as by Melanchthon, and it found an immediate response in the hearts and consciences of multitudes in Europe who were in bondage to a false gospel and crushed under the burden of rites and ceremonies. The rediscovered doctrine was none other than the sole sufficiency of God in salvation. It was not at first known as justification by faith, but it was proclaimed as the renunciation of all human works and as dependence on the grace of God alone for salvation. It made God first and supreme as the author of salvation, and it made access to Him open and free through the merits of the Lord Jesus Christ. It made faith alone the sole contact between the sinner and the Saviour. It thus put all men on a spiritual equality when they entered the presence of God, and so established the equal priesthood of all believers. It left man with sole responsibility for his destiny and the certainty of meeting with God to present his last account. It thus introduced three elements of transforming power, certainty in the matter of faith, liberty in the matter of conscience, and personal responsibility in the matter of obedience. In short, it turned theology into religion. It proved to be the substitution of one religion for another of a totally different kind, of a divine religion for a human, of the supernatural grace of God for the blind and hopeless efforts of men. And these two radically different religions gave birth to two radically different civilizations in which the feudalism and serfdom of the Dark Ages gradually gave place to the dignity of human personality, and from it the liberty and democracy of the Western world was born. This we owe to the theology of the Reformation and the outworking of those principles that Luther so forcibly brought to the surface.

BOOKS FOR FURTHER STUDY

G. Rupp, *The Righteousness of God: Luther Studies* (Hodder and Stoughton, 1953).

J. Buchanan, *The Doctrine of Justification* (Banner of Truth Trust, 1961).

CHAPTER VI

CALVIN AND THE DOCTRINE OF AUTHORITY

THE question of authority did not arise in acute form in the early Church. For the first few decades of the sub-apostolic age the Church found it sufficient to appeal to the Scriptures — mainly the Old Testament — and to the apostolic tradition, as its objective authority. The consciousness that the Spirit who descended at Pentecost was in the Church, mediating the Lordship of Christ and directing the Church's witness and teaching, gave all the internal authority necessary for the truth that it proclaimed. Between the two, the Scriptures and apostolic tradition, the early Christians were not conscious of any disharmony whatsoever. They both had their source in Christ, and we shall search in vain for any suggestion that one possesses a greater measure of inspiration and authority than the other. In fact they were but two forms of the same thing.

It was the Gnostic controversy of the second century that first compelled the Church to consider the proof of doctrine and to state more explicitly its authority for the faith it proclaimed. All its accepted sources of doctrine were attacked in turn: the Old Testament, which the Gnostics criticized as partly of God and partly of the devil; such of the New Testament writings as were in circulation, which they subjected to their own fanciful exegesis, making their meaning too vague and mystical to be of any practical value as proof of doctrine; the Creed, which was sublimated to mean almost anything or nothing; and apostolic tradition, for which the Gnostics substituted a tradition of their own, which they claimed to have come into their private possession from certain of the apostles. The great anti-Gnostic Fathers at the end of the second and beginning of the third centuries, more especially Irenaeus and Tertullian, set out to establish the 'seat' of doctrine, and place it beyond the subversive attacks of those who proclaimed their own *gnōsis* or knowledge as the way of salvation. The appeal was made to the Creed, almost certainly the Roman Creed, which is the prototype of, and almost identical with, the Apostles' Creed as we now have it; to the Scriptures, mainly of the Old Testament; and to the leaders or ' bishops ' of the apostolic churches who were holders of the true tradition of the apostles. It is true that Clement of Alexandria recognized only the Scriptures as the source of doctrine and excluded even the Creed. In this he was followed to some extent by Origen. But by the end of the third century, the Church recognized a threefold norm of authority: the Scriptures of the Old and New Testaments, for which it claimed a unique authority; the Creed as containing a summary of Scripture teaching, amplified at a later date by the findings of the Ecumenical Creeds; and the bishops of the apostolic churches.

Among the Schoolmen of the Middle Ages much emphasis was placed on reason and its power to give rational proof of the authority of the received doctrine. This was the principle on which the theological works of Thomas Aquinas, Anselm and Peter Lombard were built. The source of doctrine had by now crystallized into the Scriptures, the three Ecumenical Creeds, and the Fathers. The fundamental authority remained that of Scripture, the Creeds being regarded as summarizing Scripture, and the Fathers as explaining and interpreting it. Where the Fathers differed in doctrine from the Scriptures, they were regarded as having erred in their interpretation, and it was clearly laid down that ' a Christian is not compelled, as a necessity to salvation, to believe either as a duty or in practice, what is neither contained in the Bible, nor can be inferred as a necessary and clear consequence from the mere content of the Bible '. As regards biblical interpretation there was a growing disuse of the allegorical exegesis so common in an earlier age, and a tendency to appeal rather to the literal meaning.

In the later Scholasticism, towards the close of the Middle Ages, there developed an emphasis on the authority of the Creeds, independently of Scripture, and of the Church which, it was pointed out, formulated the Creeds and compiled the Canon of Scripture. From this it was an easy step to reach the point where the Church stood above the Bible as its only sure interpreter. Thus it came about that, while the Scriptures were formally accepted as the rule, it was the Church as the judge that was to apply the rule. Very soon, the Church, as represented by its officials, became more and more, not only the custodian of the truth, but the sole judge of what was Christian truth. It was authoritatively laid down that ' a truth is to be called Catholic, either because it is revealed of God, or contained in the divine Scripture, or because it is received by the Church, or because it is approved by the Supreme Pontiff, or because it follows from one of the above-mentioned by necessary consequence '.

THE REFORMED POSITION

It is against this conception of authority in matters of faith and life that the Reformers lodged their protest in the most emphatic and forcible way in which a protest can be lodged, by a departure from under its yoke. But when the Reformers left an authoritative Church, they were not indifferent to the supreme place of authority in religion. They merely substituted one authority for another, and for them the objective authority lay indubitably in the Scriptures. Protestant orthodoxy has indeed been defined as ' that branch of Christendom which limits the ground of religious authority to the Bible ', and William Chillingworth's dictum is well known, if not always respected: ' I tell you the Bible, and the Bible alone, is the religion of Protestants.' The two postulates of the Reformed faith, on which authority is based, are revelation and inspiration, and lacking one or the other, man has no adequate foundation for belief.

LUTHER

When Luther, standing before the Diet of Worms in 1521, was asked to retract his teaching, he answered that he would retract anything that he ' may have uttered beyond the authority of Scripture ', and declared, ' the Word of God is the greatest thing in heaven and earth, which we must all reverence '. The whole of Luther's theological system hangs on this unquestioning acceptance of the Scriptures as the Word of God. ' I will not waste a word ', he declares, ' in arguing with one who does not consider that the Scriptures are the Word of God. We ought not ', he adds, ' to dispute with a man who thus rejects first principles.'

It is true that Luther spoke strong words about some of the books of the New Testament canon: the Epistle of James was ' right strawy ', Hebrews, Jude and Revelation were not capital books. This attitude was due, not to any low ideas he had about inspiration, but to the position he took up that because some parts of Scripture were of much less value than others, they must for that reason be relegated to a secondary place. He thus attached undue importance to what he called ' the material principle ' of Scripture, and so tended to evaluate revelation in the light of its subject-matter and the doctrine revealed. To Luther the doctrine of justification by faith took first place, and any book which did not seem to him to reveal this doctrine he relegated to second place. This does not, however, reflect on Luther's doctrine of inspiration, since it could as well be argued that his conception of inspiration was particularly high, and that he was not ready to admit some books into the inspired canon without certain qualifications. To Luther ' God says ' and ' Scripture says ' are synonymous terms, and for that reason he accepted the Scriptures as the fundamental basis of authority for doctrine and life. ' The Articles of the Faith ', he said, ' are not to be built up from the words or deeds of the Fathers . . . we, on the other hand, have another rule, namely, that the Word of God should establish the Articles of Faith, and none besides, not even an angel.'

ZWINGLI

Zwingli, who differed from Luther and Calvin on so many points, was in complete agreement with them on the question of the authority of Scripture. ' The Scriptures ', he says, ' come from God, not from men, and even that God who enlightens will give thee to understand that the speech comes from God.' He was, indeed, the first in the Reformed church to see the need for a dogmatic declaration as to the place of Scripture, and his view was — posthumously — inserted in the First Helvetic Confession of 1536 to the effect that ' Canonical Scripture, the Word of God, given by the Holy Spirit, and set forth to the world by the prophets and apostles . . . alone contains perfectly all piety and the whole rule of life '.

CALVIN

It has to be recognized, however, that John Calvin did more than any other man of this epoch to clarify the thought of the Reformed Church as to the authority of the Scriptures, and his influence can be seen in the Reformed Confessions that were the theological expression of the doctrine of the Reformation. In the *Institutes of the Christian Religion* Calvin devotes chapter vi to adducing reasons for believing in the divine origin of the Scriptures, and he declares that he could produce sufficient reasons in favour of the authority of the Scripture to 'stop the obstreperous mouths of the craftiest despisers of God'. In the most unambiguous manner, the *Institutes,* which formed the greatest factor in giving doctrinal stability to the Protestantism of Europe, are themselves throughout subject to the authority of the Word of God. Calvin does not hesitate to make this the distinguishing work of the new movement that he had so strong a hand in directing. 'This is a principle which distinguishes our religion from all others,' he says, 'that we know that God has spoken to us and are fully persuaded that the prophets did not speak at their own suggestion, but that being organs of the Holy Spirit, they only uttered what they had been commanded from heaven to declare.'

CENTRES OF AUTHORITY

Though Calvin places the supreme and determining authority in the external realm, that does not mean that he recognizes no centre of authority elsewhere. The truth is that the Reformers recognized authority as both external and internal, as objective and subjective. Their position was that it rested in the Word and the Spirit, in the soul and the Church.

It is the *Word and the Spirit* that constitute and confirm authority. As the Word is the divine revelation, so the Spirit is the divine Revealer. A deposited Word, a written revelation, is a dead letter unless it is accompanied by the quickening Spirit. While it contains the truth deposited for our learning, it is ineffective to create in us the response that makes its words authoritative to us unless it is applied by the Spirit. The Roman Church had reason to learn the ineffectiveness of lifeless dogma deposited in its creeds and articles and encyclicals, and very early it had to introduce a living voice that would communicate that authority. Hence the office of the pope who can speak with authority that is unchallenged. It was but a necessary and logical step to go on to propound papal infallibility when dealing with dogma. We hold that this unfortunate expedient would have been found unnecessary had the Church remembered that the Spirit was promised to speak in the Word and communicate its authority to us. And so the supreme judge in the matter of authority ' can be no other than the voice of the Spirit in the Word '. But it must be the Word *and* the Spirit. As the Word can be lifeless without the Spirit, so the Spirit acting without the Word would lack the confirmation that we need to guarantee for us that it is in truth the Spirit of God who is dealing with us. Thus the Spirit of inspiration in the Word becomes the Spirit of illumination in us.

But, furthermore, it is the Word and the Spirit *in the soul and the Church* that completes authority. There again we have the subjective and the objective. The Word and the Spirit must make the authority felt in the soul. He is the quickening Spirit and when He quickens He uses the Word to give light to the mind, feeling to the conscience, and renewal to the will. When this happens the Spirit of God witnesses with our spirits, and the authority of God in the Word is borne home to us.

Then, again, the objective is here too. The Word and the Spirit operate with authority not only in the individual soul, but in the Church collectively. The mind of the Spirit may confidently be looked for in the body of believers, and if our experience is contradicted by the collective experience of believers, we do well to pause and ask if we have read the mind of the Spirit aright. While Protestantism has always recognized liberty of conscience and the right of private judgment, it nevertheless holds that ' individualism is not the last word in religion '. The full authority of the truth is felt only when individual illumination is supported by the concurrence of the catholic Christian experience.

Calvin was undoubtedly the first of the Reformers to place the emphasis clearly on both the objective and subjective aspects of authority, but the post-Reformation Church did not always find it easy to maintain this balance. While the theology of the English Reformation had been strongly influenced by Continental Protestantism very early in the seventeenth century, the champions of Catholic order in England were beginning to challenge the entire Calvinistic system. As an alternative they introduced a strong form of Arminianism, and in Archbishop Laud the Arminians had a resolute leader, though in reality he was more concerned with Church order than with theological belief. Arminianism, however, was branded as the characteristic view of the Royalist Party, and as a result of the Civil War it suffered eclipse, and Calvinism was again in the ascendency.

There can be no doubt but that the full flowering of the Reformed faith took place in the century following the Reformation when Puritanism in England and the Covenanting period in Scotland raised Reformed theology to its place of authority. The writings of such men as Samuel Rutherford and Thomas Boston in Scotland, and John Owen and Thomas Goodwin in England, exhibit the Reformed theology in its full development. It can, perhaps, be asserted that it was the Confession of Faith, which issued from the Westminster Assembly of Divines (1643), that marked the high-water mark of Calvinistic and Puritan theology. Though intended to serve as a basis of belief for all the Reformed churches in Europe, it was, in the event, accepted only by the Church of Scotland, and from then it became the subordinate standard of the Presbyterian churches throughout the world. Calvin's *Institutes* apart, it is the clearest reproduction in Confessional form of the theology of the Reformation, and the guiding principle that animated the whole was the supreme authority of the Word of God in the formation of Christian character as well as in the guidance of Christian conduct. Combining the theological and the practical as does perhaps no other Confession, ancient or modern, it is, in compact form, the greatest manual of religion that the Reformation has produced. And it bears indelibly the distinctive mark of English Puritanism at its strongest and clearest.

Puritanism, however, was miscellaneous in its theological output. It concentrated strongly on the doctrine of salvation in the realm of individual experience. The fact that it was not practically organized, like Presbyterianism in Scotland, but was represented largely by a fugitive church, militated against the formation of an orderly theology. As it is, the theological output of Puritanism that has come down to us may still be of use as bridging the gulf between doctrinal Calvinism and introspective piety.

Puritanism survived in America after it had been crushed in Britain, so that it was still possible to find a theologian of the stature of Jonathan Edwards in New England in the middle of the eighteenth century. In England the Puritans had no comparable successors after the catastrophe of 1662 when they were silenced by an Act of Parliament. The Methodism of the Wesleys was an Arminianized form of evangelicalism, though in the preaching of their contemporary, George Whitefield, the note of Calvinism was still clearly struck.

FOR FURTHER STUDY

J. Murray, *Calvin on Scripture and Divine Sovereignty* (Baker Book House, 1961).

G. R. Cragg, *From Puritanism to the Age of Reason, 1660-1700.*

CHAPTER VII

SCHLEIERMACHER AND THE DOCTRINES OF MODERN THEOLOGY

THE era of modern theology is considered to have begun with the German theologian Friedrich Schleiermacher (1768-1834), who is generally spoken of as the father of modern theology. The reason for this lies in the fact that with Schleiermacher theology adopted a new approach and was based on new principles. Assailed by philosophical scepticism under Locke and Hume, and by scientific materialism as a product of the hypotheses of Darwin, religion was placed on the defensive as its foundations were crumbling under the new learning. The reaction was to turn away from philosophical arguments for theistic belief, and lay the foundations of theology in the experience, feelings and moral drives of men. Theology thus took up an anthropological and humanistic starting point. Schleiermacher, in his attempt to rehabilitate religion by placing it on the basis of the religious consciousness, adopted the method of inquiring, not what God said from without, but what the Christian consciousness said from within. The new approach to belief in God was thus from the standpoint of man's inner life and experience, and not from the authority of divine revelation.

It could be seen, however, that theology resting on something as fluid and subjective as the Christian consciousness could not deal with universally valid truth and could have little permanent form. It is to that extent, perhaps, a misnomer to speak of the 'doctrines' of modern theology.

Theology under Schleiermacher degenerated into mere humanism, the study of psychology and of comparative religions took over from the study of divine revelation in the Scriptures, and the leaders of the Church felt that some rethinking would have to be done if religion was to survive.

LIBERAL THEOLOGY

Though the new trend had its peril in its subservance to philosophy and science, it had the merit, in the eyes of beleagured theologians, that it introduced a methodology that could be used in the rebuilding of theology on new foundations. The one who saw this most clearly was the German teacher Albrecht Ritschl (1822-1889). Acutely aware of the dangers of over-subjectivism on the one hand, and of dependence upon philosophy and physical science on the other, Ritschl introduced his own theory of religious knowledge as based on what he called judgment of values. In doing this Ritschl was really setting up a dualism between judgment of knowledge and judgment of values, between the religious and the theoretical, not allowing the one to be influenced by the other. On this principle, what was valid as religious knowledge was not necessarily valid on the plane of theoretical thinking. We have become very familiar with this dichotomy in the theological thinking of today, but for Ritschl it had the result of freeing theology from dependence upon philosophy and nature-knowledge. Religious thought was distinguished from theoretical thought in that it moved in an independent judgment of values, and in this Ritschl was trying to give an interpretation of Christianity that would commend the gospel to the mind and heart of the age.

Judgment of Values

When it is recognized that this judgment of values was necessarily dependent on an act of the will which determines values, it can be seen that it was but the subjectivism of Schleiermacher in a new guise, resting the validity of religious judgment on the will rather than on the feelings. In both cases there was introduced into our religious expression an element in which it was not clear how much was objective reality, and how much subjective construction. Ordinarily we accept that knowledge implies objective data from which the mind makes its value judgments and therefore that there can be no conflict between judgments of values and judgments of existence; both enter into our knowledge and are complements of each other, provided the values are real values and the presentation of them true.

Kingdom of God Teaching

With this new weapon Ritschl set about to reconstruct theology. The teaching of Christ he found to consist mainly in teaching on the kingdom of God, and he held that the apostles lapsed from their Master's point of view in losing hold of His idea of the kingdom of God. But the 'value' of the kingdom of God to Ritschl was that of an association of moral beings in which the members act reciprocally from the motive of love, love being defined simply and loosely as adopting the ends of others as their own, the exact nature of the ends being left undefined. Christ Himself was simply a uniquely constituted and exceptionally endowed man who has for us 'the value of God'. How a purely human being can have for us the value of God is not defined beyond the assurance that Christ is 'a revelation organ of God'. The traditional doctrines about the Person of Christ are to be accepted as 'thoughts of faith', and so there emerges the now familiar dichotomy between the 'Christ of faith' and the 'Jesus of history'.

Liberal Positions

The positions adopted by the later Liberalism were distinguished by the emphasis placed on the immanence of God to the almost complete neglect of His transcendence, the disparagement of inscript orated revelation and therefore of biblical authority, a preoccupation with the Jesus of history as distinct from the Christ of theology, and the emergence of a social gospel as the distinctive message of Christianity to the almost complete neglect of the redemptive message of the New Testament.

All of these were derived, directly or indirectly, from the 'value judgments' introduced by Albrecht Ritschl, and defective as his theological presuppositions appear to us, they set the norm for theology for a full century, and established a methodology that the theologians of the nineteenth and early twentieth centuries were to adopt. Ritschlianism thus became the common label for Liberal theology until the intrusion of Karl Barth into the theological arena had opened up for the Liberal theologians the possibility of theology remaining modern and finding expression in other categories.

DIALECTICAL THEOLOGY

This will always be associated with the name of the Swiss-German theologian Karl Barth (1886-1968), though many of his positions had been anticipated by such men as Macleod Campbell, Baron von Hugel, and especially P. T. Forsyth.

Background

The rise of the new theology was inevitable if we accept the inevitability of the swing of the pendulum from one extreme to the other. Liberal frontiers were in a fluid state, and Liberalism itself was more a spirit or a methodology than a coherent system. The outbreak of the First World War — in which Germany and the English-speaking world were on opposite sides — and the bestiality that accompanied it gave a shattering blow to the theological optimism that was based on the inevitability of human progress. There was also the fact that a new ideology in the form of Communism had arisen to challenge the old world and its ideas, and for this the vagaries of Liberalism were no match.

It was then that the voice of Karl Barth broke on a weary and disillusioned age, calling men to a transcendent God, a supernatural revelation, and a living experience of divine grace. We are told that his *Römerbrief* — an exposition of the Epistle to the Romans — in 1919 'fell like a bombshell on the playground of the theologians' (Althaus). It not only asserted the transcendence of God, but disclaimed the possibility of man attaining to any knowledge of God-in-Himself. At the same time it disowned proposition and concept as media of divine revelation. It was now clear that behind the Commentary there lay themes familiar to all who were acquainted with Calvin and the other Reformers, such as the divine initiative in man's redemption, the wrath of God, man's sinfulness, and miraculous redemptive revelation, and it was equally clear that it indicated a break with the old Liberalism that had prevailed since Ritschl's day. It asserted that Christianity is not just one religion among many, but the response to the Word of God as it encounters man.

With these themes, asserted with startling boldness and in provocative language, men thought that the theology of the Reformation was breaking in upon the world again with freshness and authority, and Conservative theologians who were holding the fort in diminishing numbers took new courage. But all too soon it became apparent that a reassessment would have to be made. What was being proclaimed in the accents of orthodoxy was turning out to be but a new Modernism rather than the old Evangelicalism.

But it took hold. Very rapidly Karl Barth became the leader of a new school, and as such gathered around him a circle of younger men who gave him every homage even when, as it turned out, they later diverged very considerably from his positions.

New Terms

Barth introduced into our theological vocabulary terms that were not always easy to understand and interpret, though many of them had been more or less familiar to students of the Danish philosopher and metaphysician, Soren Kierkegaard. 'Existential' and ' dialectical ' became the most permanent of these, and it is by the second that Barth's theology comes to be distinguished from the schools of thought before and after him. The dialectical relationship takes many forms too numerous and complex to follow out in this brief survey. The main distinction between it and evangelical orthodoxy is that while orthodoxy stands for direct revelation, dialecticalism stands for indirect. This one conception results in a complete reinterpretation of Scripture and revelation in relation to reason and history.

Extreme Transcendence

Barthian theology throughout represents a somewhat violent reaction against the extreme positions of Liberalism. In his attempt to emphasize the transcendence of God, Barth succeeds in putting God beyond the reach of all human understanding and human faculties. God was the ' wholly other ' to man; He must not be ' identified with anything we name or experience, or conceive, or worship as God '. While this was a rebound from the Liberal conception of the continuity of man with God, it was a rebound that took us beyond all revelation of God. It is this extreme presentation of the transcendence of God to the complete neglect of His immanence that casts its shadow over the whole of Barth's theology and makes it, in so many ways, a contradiction of what the Church over the centuries accepted as the biblical presentation of the divine Being.

Super-history

It is because of his over-emphasis on transcendence that Barth holds that revelation cannot take place in history and cannot be given in conceptual forms that are open to human cognition.

When Barth still asserts that revelation can be historical, he means that revelation can take place in another dimension than ordinary history, in what he calls super-history. This has serious consequences in dealing with the historical Christ, leading Barth to say that the revelation of Christ is not directly identical with Jesus of Nazareth, the Jesus of history. This compels him to hold that the historical crucifixion and resurrection have no redemptive objectivity.

Since revelation is, by Barthian definition, supra-historical, no book can possibly enshrine that revelation. The Bible is therefore not the revelation, but a witness to the revelation, a human witness to a divine revelation. For that reason the Scriptures must partake of all the limitations and deficiencies of a human witness. It is only when we meet God there in divine-human encounter that the Scripture becomes divine revelation and its fallible propositions become vehicles of divine truth to us. When this divine-human encounter is over, the Scriptures are merely what they were before, fallible human witness. This renders the Scriptures worthless as the source of any trustworthy knowledge of God and must be regarded as such by all who have not had this encounter.

From this it can be seen how far Barth has departed from conservative evangelical positions. The fact that revelation is confined to divine-human encounter must mean that man's conception of God is framed in terms of his own experience, and is not subject to the corrective of an objective revelation. Further, the dichotomy between ordinary history and super-history means that man's experience of conversion, and all that leads up to it, must be placed outside ordinary history to which man's other experiences belong. This leads to the complete alienation of Christian culture from Christian theology, so that, for example, there can be no common ground between science and religion.

NEO-LIBERAL THEOLOGY

There were several movements, in more than one sphere, that led to the disintegration of classical Liberalism. We have already noted that the older Modernism had little to say to a world striving to emerge from the agony of two wars. Religion had lost its authority to speak to the real condition of man. Moreover, Liberal theology was found to be utterly inadequate to deal with the facts of revealed religion as given in the Scriptures. Thinking men came to realize that there was more to the Bible than the identification of the documents of which it is composed, which was the self-appointed province of Source Criticism to investigate.

Barthian and Pre-Barthian Influence

The influence of Karl Barth, however, contributed to the reconstruction of Liberal theology more than any other factor. Barth recalled theologians to a reconsideration of their faith as a religion of revelation, but since he did not seriously disturb the foundations on which the old Liberalism had been reared, it will be seen that the new Liberalism absorbed Barthianism as a corrective rather than accepted it as an alternative. Non-evangelical spokesmen could now talk of the Bible as ' the normative witness to Christ ' and as ' inspired ', even when they refused to accept the controlling premise of evangelical Christianity as to the supreme authority of Scripture.

It is quite apparent that pre-Barthian theologians lent a hand in this reconstruction, notably such men as P. T. Forsyth, James Denney, and James Orr, all of whom sounded a strongly conservative note — with certain aberrations — within the Liberal camp.

Positions of Neo-Liberalism

Neo-Liberalism took up positions that were more akin to the old Conservatism than to the old Liberalism. It emphasized the transcendence of God and laid stress on man's sinful state and the bondage it entails. By whatever name sin was spoken of, it was a condition that called for redemption. And there was a recognition that man must be redeemed from outside himself, that it must be an operation of grace. There was an apparent break with the old Liberalism that regarded human nature as continuous with the divine, that regarded sin as a mere neurosis and its remedy a matter for the psychiatrist to take in hand. All this was quietly set aside, and the Scripture was once again accepted as a word from God to man in his predicament.

But the new Liberalism, whether it be termed Neo-orthodoxy or Neo-Liberalism, accepted essentially the methodology of the older school and reared its superstructure upon a Bible subjected to the acid tests of literary, historical and scientific criticism.

It not so much disowned the assumptions of the old school as superseded them as no longer of relevance to contemporary man. Theology had passed into the post-critical period.

The Historical Method

There was notably a shift now in relation to the New Testament documents which were being accepted, not as historical narratives, but as community documents that reflected the faith of the Church a full century after the crucifixion. It thus replaced the Jesus of history by the kerygmatic Christ, that is, the Christ which the faith of the early Church had constructed and proclaimed in its message. This was indeed a reorientation, since formerly the Jesus of history filled the entire content of faith and the New Testament interpretation of Him was regarded as irrelevant for us. Now it was the interpretation of the Church that mattered.

This meant that our knowledge of Christ is not dependent on what can be known about the historical life of Christ, and our faith rests on something or someone other than that presented in New Testament documents. Further, we are reminded that our knowledge of the authoritative words of Christ is not limited to what can be established as Jesus' words, and so a distinction has to be made between the words of Jesus and the words of Christ. In addition to this, the truth about the meaning of Christ does not depend on what can be discovered as the way in which Jesus thought of the meaning of His career, so that the meaning of Christ is not identical with what was present in the self-consciousness of Jesus. Thus, as we are not allowed to place the saving event within the limits of Christ's historical career, so we are not allowed to interpret the event in terms of ideas that were present in Jesus' mind.

It can be clearly seen that under the criticism adopted by the so-called Historical Method, the roots of Christianity are cut from history and from any historical connection with the Person of Jesus Christ. But with our developing knowledge of the apostolic period, the Historical Method is being increasingly discredited as in fact unhistorical. The assignment of the Gospels to a late date is not now generally accepted, and the linguistic argument offered in proof of a late date is greatly weakened by the evidence of the Dead Sea Scrolls. The early Church was fully alive to the fact that a sharp line of demarcation separated it from the apostolic period, and it was careful in accepting as authoritative for its faith only what bore the imprimatur of the apostles or those in close touch with them. The evidence is convincing that it was not the early Church that gave us the New Testament Scriptures, but that it was the New Testament writings which called the Church into being, separated it from the world, and made clear to it its vocation as a witness to its Lord.

EXISTENTIAL THEOLOGY

Philosophical Existentialism began with Soren Kierkegaard and in later years many of its concepts have come to be used in a theological setting. Existentialism in itself implies a denial of God's reality, since it grants no existence outside man's experience. But existentialist theologians, in common with their master Rudolf Bultmann (b. 1884), repudiate any denial of the reality of God. Its main characteristic as popularized by Bultmann is that it regards the miraculous in religion as myth, and holds that the supernatural is merely a pointer to elements of experience that may transcend scientific inquiry.

When Karl Barth published in 1919 his *Römerbrief* it was seen that his dialectical theology refused to root faith in objective history and objective knowledge. Bultmann took over Barth's dialectical approach and used it in his application of Form Criticism (*Formgeschichte*) and Existentialism (*Existenz*). While existential theology was willing to travel so far with Dialecticalism, it extended the emphasis on personal encounter, as over against propositional revelation, to the point of dismissing all historical props and logical supports for faith. Bultmann held that modern science required a non-miraculous understanding of the New Testament and that faith demanded no historical foundation beyond postulating the historical existence of Christ. The New Testament was thus to be understood existentially, and a sharp cleavage was drawn between existential and historical revelation.

The Demythologizing Programme

According to Bultmann's interpretation, the New Testament writers thought in terms of the world-view current in their time, and since this world-view is mythological throughout, and so utterly alien to the thought of a scientific age, his concern is that the gospel should be made intelligible and acceptable to modern man. In order to do this it must be released from its mythological framework.

To Bultmann, however, the process of demythologizing does not mean the complete abandonment of the New Testament so much as its reinterpretation. For him this is the only alternative to either accepting or rejecting the New Testament world-thought. He considers it is, therefore, our duty to penetrate through the myth framework to the reality that the New Testament writers sought to present. He holds that there is a valid biblical message which need not be abandoned when the biblical world-view is set aside. This is the *kerygma*, the vital message of the Scriptures, which must be removed from its mythological setting, and by the process of demythologization the biblical message is set free to be presented to the present age.

The Content of the Christian Faith

It will not be surprising that from this approach very little is left of the historic content of the Christian faith. When everything is eliminated that is an invasion of the supernatural, or that ' confuses ' the saving activity of God with a literal event, past or future, such doctrines as the sinlessness of Christ, the supernatural atonement, the resurrection and ascension and coming judgment, must be abandoned. According to Bultmann it is of no serious moment to faith whether the traditions enshrined in the Gospels are historical or not, since faith cannot be based on history and has little or no interest in a Christ after the flesh. Preoccupation with a historical Jesus is, he says, actually destructive of Chrisitanity, and merely leads to a ' Jesus cult '. Yet, strange as it may seem to us, the unhistorical as well as the historical both constitute the ' object of faith ', in which case faith may, in many instances, be producing the event, rather than the event producing the faith.

It is clear that Bultmann ignores the biblical standpoint that God has acted in history for our salvation, or that anything that has happened in history is essential to God's redemptive dealings with man in history. Christianity is thus unhistorical. But, more, if we eliminate the supernatural from Christianity it falls into the category of general religion and is utterly inadequate to meet man's longing to know his own relation to the supernatural, and be placed in real living contact with it.

SECULAR THEOLOGY

The beginning of the revolt against Existential Theology could be discerned in the period between 1955 and 1960. It was pointed out that the Jesus of Bultmannian existentialism evaporated into a figure that had little relation to history, with the result that the New Testament gospel was not essentially different from early Gnostic attempts to present a doctrinal Christianity. There began, therefore, a new attempt to engage in the quest of the historical Jesus, and to relate the gospel and its theology in some way with His historical appearing. Clearly there must be some connection between the historical Jesus and the content of the Christian faith, and the nature and extent of this connection give scope for a wide variety of standpoints.

Of all the alternatives to Bultmannian theology, the most vigorous is that associated with Paul Tillich (1886-1964) under the name of Secular Theology. This may well be a misnomer. Secular, properly understood, does not connote irreligion, but merely a period of time, an age. It is only in more recent times, when many areas of human life and thought came to be regarded as outside the purview of religion, that secular was accepted as the antonym of sacred or religious. This led to religion in general, and Christianity in particular, being regarded as merely a matter of private practice, quite unrelated to human affairs in general. It is here that the new terminology came into use to connote a religion that took to do with the affairs of time and of everyday life. Hence secular religion, which dealt only with the here and now and had no authority outside the strictly mundane level. The reality of a transcendental sphere was outside its scope, only human beings and their relationships mattered.

This has secured for it many titles, some of them deliberately chosen to alarm and shock, such as 'religionless Christianity', 'God is dead theology', and 'religion without God'. It is apparent, on closer acquaintance, that 'religionless' Christianity refers more to formal religion, or what we would call 'religiosity', rather than to vital religion, and as such it merely claims to dispense with the outward trappings or the common expressions of religion, such as we find in public prayer and worship, which are thought to be alien to the thought and culture of the present age, and as such a hindrance rather than a help. But even so, to cut off Christianity from its recognized expressions in piety and worship is like stripping a tree of its leaves and so leading to its decay and death.

Similarly, 'religion without God' has to be looked at in its context of 'man come of age'. Bonhoeffer remarks: 'Man has learned to cope with all questions of importance without recourse to God as a working hypothesis.' While this has been for long claimed in matters of science, art, ethics, etc., only now is it being claimed for religion also, for 'it is becoming evident', as Bonhoeffer concludes, 'that everything gets along without God just as before'.

This in turn has led to the startling caption 'The Death of God Theology', which does not presume to pass judgment on whether God is in fact dead or not, but on the fact that as far as man is concerned God is so completely absent that He is as good as dead. The death of God theology is thus a theology from which God is absent, even as a working hypothesis, since the secularity of our culture has rendered the term 'God' meaningless. The essential Christian message, it is thought, can be expressed without the use of the term 'God' or its equivalents, for if God refers to some sort of reality beyond the ordinary processes of the world, it is not possible to define what we are talking about. Rather is it an oblique way of referring to certain attitudes and feelings and expectations, and not to any objective reality. It is therefore meaningless to use the term 'God' at all. This has given rise to the charge that He is merely a 'God of the gaps', an expedient to bridge over the gaps in our knowledge and understanding, a bridge that becomes less and less necessary as our knowledge develops.

Thus while Bultmann had sought to deal with the realities of the Christian faith by a process of demythologizing, so now Tillich and his followers find it logical to claim that 'God' is a religious symbol, a product of myth and cult. What has begun as a non-miraculous Christianity now ends as a non-theistic Christianity, whose final goal is nihilism.

OTHER DEVELOPMENTS

It falls now to trace, in a wider pattern, the direction in which the tide of New Testament scholarship in Europe seems to be flowing.

The newer Heilsgeschichte School, as distinct from the old

Erlangen School, emerges in opposition to the kerygmatic emphasis of the last decade that emphasized the Christ of faith to the almost complete neglect of the historical Jesus. While it postulated that Christ did exist as a historical figure, it was not interested in who or what He was since it substituted the Christ of experience for the Jesus of history. The new Continental school, led by Oscar Cullmann, Adolf Köberle, Wolfhardt Pannenberg, Anders Nygren, and Helmut Thielicke, and others of a conservative standpoint, asserts the historical character of divine revelation and recognizes that the saving events of biblical history support the ground of Christian faith.

They join issue with Bultmann at more than one point and hold that the historical Jesus must be regarded as vitally important for all New Testament studies. They disregard Bultmann's view that the Gospels of Jesus and most other New Testament writings were influenced by Hellenistic and Gnostic emphases and they stress the Palestinian and Judean character of these writings and point to the evidence supplied by the Dead Sea Scrolls in support of this. In contrast to Bultmann's claim that existential understanding of the New Testament is the task of exegesis, the Gospels are now being recognized again as the communication of knowledge about God rather than merely knowledge about ourselves. The claim made by Form Criticism that the New Testament does not provide a reliable report of the historical Jesus is now weakening before a recognition of the continuity of the teaching of the primitive Church with that of Jesus and the apostles.

Divine revelation and redemption are now being acknowledged as objective historical realities, facts which are open to the scrutiny of historical students as the ordinary facts of history are. There is also a new emphasis on the Old Testament as providing the revelational background of the New in which it found its fulfilment. The meaning of the events of sacred history is once again accepted as divinely given.

Among continental scholars Oscar Cullmann of Basel most nearly approximates traditional positions in holding that authentic Christian faith presupposes acceptance of the historical fact that Jesus of Nazareth regarded Himself as the Messiah, and he recognizes the reality of revelation in both the event and its interpretation. He claims indeed that Jesus Himself was the first interpreter of the events, and that only afterwards did the apostles bring to mind what He had told them. Christ is thus behind the reinterpretation of the *kerygma* by the New Testament writers. What is not recognized by the Heilsgeschichte school — to which Cullmann refers rather disparagingly as the ' magic wand to solve biblical and theological mysteries ' — is that revelation consists not merely in deeds and their interpretation, but also in knowledge about God's nature and character.

There is also to be noted a growing recognition, among Continental scholars, of revelation as truth and not merely as history. Adolf Köberle of Tübingen attacks the particular dialectical-existential emphasis on revelation and claims that ' what God has done, and what He has said, is fully as important as what God is doing and is saying, and, in fact, is the presupposition of what He is doing and saying '.

Wolfhardt Pannenberg of Mainz, one of Barth's former students, speaks sharply of the vacillation of the dialectical theologians in regard to the truth of revelation. He asserts: ' Their denial of the objectivity of revelation is a threat to the very reality of revelation.' Though Pannenberg insists that revelation is objective in the form of historical events, he does not, however, recognize that it is given in divinely inspired propositions. But he realizes that the Scriptures contain not only a theology of revelation, but revelation in the form of truth that is universally accessible and universally valid whether we exercise a personal decision for or against it. Pannenberg likewise joins in the attack upon the dialectical formulation of transcendence from which, as we have already seen, many of the peculiarities and inconsistences of Barthian theology spring.

Anders Nygren of Lund joins with Oscar Cullmann in his dissociation from the Barthian exaggeration of the qualitative difference between eternity and time, involving, as it does, a concept of revelation that takes no account of its relation to nature, history and conscience.

Helmut Thielicke of Hamburg stresses that Barth's notion of the revelation of God as known only in individual response deprives the world at large of the truth by which it will eventually be judged.

While these are trends in the direction of a more conservative approach to revelation and the theology derived from it which we cannot but welcome, we would stress that the complete authority of Scripture for faith and life is still the main issue.

The bedrock of evangelical Christianity is still, as it has always been, the Bible, and the fate of Christianity is inseparable from the fate of the Bible. We accept, however, the assessment of one of our American theologians that the evangelical witness has before it today a twofold task, coping with misunderstandings of its positions, and clarifying the implications of its viewpoints. Conservative theologians must bend their energies and scholarships to this two-fold task in the conviction that though biblical supernaturalness is the historic faith of Christianity and the only theology that can lead to the regeneration of human nature, we are still called upon to ' give a reason for the hope that is in us '.

133/69